PURITAN PAPERBACKS

*Heaven Taken by Storm, or
The Christian Soldier*

Thomas Watson

c. 1620–1686

Thomas Watson was probably born in Yorkshire, although the exact place and date of his birth are unknown. He studied at Emmanuel College, Cambridge (BA, 1639; MA, 1642), where he was apparently a diligent student. Certainly his intellect is apparent in his writings, which show a profound grasp of the English language, as well as a solid understanding of Hebrew, Greek, and Latin. He quotes from the early church fathers, and his familiarity with the breadth of the scriptural canon is stunning.

In 1646 Watson went to St Stephen's, Walbrook, London, where he served as lecturer for about ten years, and then as rector for another six years. Here he served with 'great diligence and assiduity. … The church was constantly filled, for the fame and popularity of the preacher were deservedly great' (C. H. Spurgeon).

With the Act of Uniformity in 1662, Watson was ejected from his pastorate, although he continued to preach in private whenever he had the opportunity. After the Declaration of Indulgence took effect in 1672, Watson obtained a license for Crosby Hall, Bishopsgate, which belonged to Sir John Langham, a patron of nonconformists. Watson preached there for three years before Stephen Charnock joined him. They ministered together until Charnock's death in 1680.

Watson kept working until his health failed. He then retired to Barnston, in Essex, where he died suddenly in 1686 while engaged in private prayer.

Thomas Watson

Heaven Taken by Storm

or,

The Christian Soldier

*Showing the Holy Violence a Christian is
to Put Forth in the Pursuit after Glory*

I press toward the mark.—Phil. 3:14.

THE BANNER OF TRUTH TRUST

THE BANNER OF TRUTH TRUST

Head Office
3 Murrayfield Road
Edinburgh, EH12 6EL
UK

North America Office
610 Alexander Spring Road
Carlisle, PA 17015
USA

banneroftruth.org

First published 1669
First Banner of Truth edition 2025
Text based on the second London edition revised and corrected
by Rev. Mr Armstrong, Rector of St Michael, Crooked-Lane

© The Banner of Truth Trust 2025

*

ISBN
Print: 978 1 80040 552 3
Epub: 978 1 80040 553 0

*

Typeset in 10/13 Minion Pro at
The Banner of Truth Trust, Edinburgh

Printed in the USA by
Versa Press Inc.,
East Peoria, IL.

Contents

Introduction: Heaven is to be Taken by Force or Violence ... 1

    I. The preface or introduction ... 2

    II. The matter in the text ... 3

    Doctrine: The right way to take heaven is by storm: or thus, None get into heaven but violent ones. ... 4

    I. Application to magistrates ... 4

    II. Application to Christians ... 5

        1. What this violence is not ... 5

        2. What this violence is ... 7

        3. What does this violence imply? ... 9

            (1) Resolution of will ... 9

            (2) Vigour of the affections ... 10

            (3) Strength of endeavour ... 10

        4. In what ways must the Christian offer violence? ... 11

        Four ways: to Self, Satan, the World, and Heaven ... 11

I.	**He Must Offer Violence to Himself**	11
	1. Mortification of sin	11
	2. Provocation to duty	13
	(1) Need to stir ourselves up to duty	14
	(2) What it is to stir ourselves up to duty	14
	(3) Seven duties to be violently engaged in:	15
	1st. Reading of the word	15
	2nd. Hearing of the word	19
	3rd. Prayer	21
	4th. Meditation	26
	5th. Self-examination	35
	6th. Religious sanctifying of the Lord's day	40
	7th. Holy conference	44
II.	**We Must Offer Violence to Satan**	47
	1. To Satan's violence	47
	2. To Satan's treachery	47
	1. By faith	49
	2. By prayer	49
III.	**We Must Offer Violence to the World**	50
	1. The world is deceitful.	51
	2. The world is defiling.	52

3. The world is perishing.	52
IV. We Must Offer Violence to Heaven	52
Scripture allegories that imply violence:	52
1. Striving	52
2. Wrestling	52
3. Running	52
Where is this holy violence to be found?	53
Reasons why this holy violence is necessary:	53
1. God's indispensable command	53
2. God's decree	53
3. The difficulty of the work	54
4. The violence of the opposition	54
5. The vital importance of the matter	54
(1) What we shall save? A precious soul	54
(2) What we shall gain? A kingdom	55
Reproofs Arising from the Text	59
1. To the slothful	59
2. To the formalist	61
3. To the violent in a bad sense	62
4. To backsliders and apostates	65
5. To procrastinators	72
6. To mockers	73

7. To violent opposers	73

Questions for Self-Examination — 74

1. Do we strive with our hearts to get them into a holy frame?	74
2. Do we set time apart to call ourselves to account, and try our evidences for heaven?	75
3. Do we use violence in prayer?	75
4. Do we thirst for the living God?	75
5. Are we skilled in self-denial?	75
6. Are we lovers of God?	75
7. Do we keep our spiritual watch?	75
8. Do we press after further degrees of sanctity?	76
9. Is there a holy emulation in us?	76
10. Are we got above the world?	76
11. Do we set ourselves always under God's eye?	76

Objections to this Duty — 77

1. We have no power of ourselves to save ourselves.	77
2. This offering violence is hard, and I shall never be able to go through it.	78
3. If I put myself upon this violent exercise in religion, then I shall lose that pleasure I have in my sin, etc.	79

CONTENTS

4. I would use this violence for heaven, but I shall expose myself to the censure and scorn of others. — 82

5. If I use this holy violence, and turn religious, then I shall lose such yearly profits which my sin hath brought in. — 83

6. But I have so much business in the world that I can find no time for this holy violence. — 83

Further Exhortations — 85

1. Consider the deplorable condition we are in by nature – a state of misery and damnation; therefore what violence should we use to get out of it! — 85

2. It is possible that in the use of means we may arrive at happiness. — 85

3. This violence for heaven is the grand business of our lives: what did we come into the world for else? — 86

4. How violent are the wicked in ways of sin! — 87

5. This holy violence hath much delight mingled with it. — 88

6. This violence and activity of spirit in religion, puts a lustre upon a Christian. — 89

7. How violent was Christ about our salvation! — 89

8. This holy violence brings rest. — 89

9. If we use what violence we are able, God will help us. 89

10. This blessed violence in religion would be preventative of much sin. 90

11. The folly of such as are violent for the world, but not for the kingdom above 90

12. This violence is for a kingdom. 91

13. The more violence we have used for heaven, the sweeter heaven will be when we come there. 94

14. The more violence we put forth in religion, the greater measure of glory we shall have. 95

15. Upon our violence for the kingdom, God hath promised mercy. 95

16. This holy violence will not hinder men in their secular employments. 97

17. There is but a short space of time granted us, therefore work the harder for heaven before it be too late. 98

18. A man's personal day of grace may be short. 99

19. If you neglect the offering violence now, there will be no help for you after death. 100

20. How without all apology will you be left, if you neglect this violence for heaven! 101

21. What a vexation it will be at the last to lose the kingdom of glory for want of a little violence!	102
22. The examples of the saints of old, who have taken heaven by force.	102
23. If the saints with all their violence have much ado to get to heaven, how shall they come there who use no violence?	103
24. This sweating for heaven is not to endure long.	104
25. If you are not violent for heaven, you walk contrary to your own prayers.	104
26. This holy and blessed violence would make Christians willing to die.	105
27. If you will either sit still, or keep your sweat for something else than heaven, know, there is a time shortly coming when you will wish you had used this violence.	105
A Necessary Cautionary Note	106
Though we shall not obtain the kingdom without violence, yet not for our violence.	106
Rules and Directions for Getting this Violence for Heaven	107
1. Take heed of those things which will hinder this violence for heaven:	107
(1) Take heed of unbelief.	107

(2) Take heed of puzzling your thoughts about election.	108
(3) Take heed of too much violence after the world.	109
(4) Take heed of indulging any lust.	110
(5) Take heed of despondency of spirit.	111
(6) Take heed of a supine, lazy temper.	112
(7) Take heed of consulting with flesh and blood.	112
(8) Take heed of listening to the voice of such carnal friends as would call you off from this blessed violence.	113
(9) Take heed of setting up your stay in the lowest pitch of grace.	115
(10) Take heed of this opinion that it is not so hard to get the kingdom; less violence will serve turn.	115
2. Use those means which will promote this holy violence:	116
(1) Keep up daily prayer.	116
(2) Get under lively preaching.	116
(3) Get your hearts filled with love to religion.	117
(4) Warm yourselves at this fire of love.	117
(5) Be vigilant.	117
(6) Bind your heart to God by sacred vows.	118

(7) Be sure you make going to heaven your business.	118
(8) Have heaven continually in your eye.	118
(9) Keep company with such as are violent.	119
(10) Never leave till you have the Spirit.	120

Concluding Applications — 120

To aged Christians. — 120

To violent Christians. — 121

To fearful and weak Christians. — 122

Heaven Taken by Storm,

or,

The Christian Soldier

'The kingdom of heaven suffereth violence, and the violent take it by force.' – Matt. 11:12.

Introduction:
Heaven is to be Taken by Force or Violence

JOHN BAPTIST, hearing in prison the fame of Christ, sends two of his disciples to him with this question, 'Art thou he that should come, or do we look for another?' (Matt. 11:3). Not (as Tertullian thinks) that John Baptist knew not that Jesus Christ was the true Messiah; for he was confirmed in this both by the Spirit of God and by a sign from heaven (John 1:33). But John Baptist hereby endeavoured to correct the ignorance of his own disciples, who had a greater respect for him than for Christ.

In the fourth verse Christ answers their question: 'Go and show John again those things which ye do hear and see; the blind receive their sight, the lame walk, the lepers are cleansed,' etc. Jesus Christ demonstrates himself to be the true Messiah by his miracles which were real and ocular proofs of his divinity. John's disciples being departed, Christ falls into a high eulogium and commendation of John Baptist: 'What went ye out into the wilderness to see, a reed, shaken with the wind?' (Matt. 11:7). As if Christ had said, John Baptist was no inconstant man, fluctuating in his mind and being shaken as a reed from one opinion to another. He was no Reuben, 'unstable as water,' but was fixed and resolute in religion, and a prison could make no alteration in him.

'But what went ye out for to see? A man clothed in soft raiment?' (verse 8). John did not indulge his senses; he wore not silks, but camels' hair; nor did he affect to live at court, but in a wilderness (Matt. 3:3, 4).

Again, Christ commends John as being his forerunner, 'who prepared the way before him' (verse 10). He was the morning star which did precede the sun of righteousness; and that Christ might sufficiently honour this holy man, he doth not only parallel him with, but prefer him before, the chief of the prophets. 'What went ye out for to see? A prophet? yea, I say unto you, and more than a prophet … Among them that are born of women, there hath not risen a greater than John the Baptist' (verses 9, 11). He was eminent both for dignity of office and perspicuity of doctrine. And so the text is ushered in: 'from the days of John the Baptist, until now, the kingdom of heaven suffereth violence, and the violent take it by force.' In which words there is:

I. The preface or introduction

'From the days of John the Baptist until now.' John Baptist was a zealous preacher, a 'Boanerges' or son of thunder,

and after his preaching people began to be awakened out of their sins.

Hence learn what kind of ministry is like to do most good, namely, that which works upon the consciences of men. John Baptist did lift up his voice like a trumpet, he preached the doctrine of repentance with power: 'Repent, for the kingdom of heaven is at hand' (Matt. 3:2). He came hewing and cutting down men's sins, and afterwards preached Christ to them. First he poured in the vinegar of the law, then the wine of the gospel. This was that preaching which made men studiously seek after heaven. John did not so much preach to please, as to profit; he chose rather to discover men's sins, than to show his own eloquence. That is the best looking-glass, not which is most gilded, but which shows the truest face. That preaching is to be preferred which makes the truest discovery of men's sins, and shows them their hearts. John Baptist 'was a burning and shining light'; he did burn in his doctrine, and shine in his life; and from that time men pressed into heaven. Peter (who was filled with a spirit of zeal), having humbled his hearers for their sins, and opened to them a fountain in Christ's blood, they were then 'pricked at their heart' (Acts 2:37). 'Tis the greatest mercy to have a soul-searching ministry. If one had a desperate wound, he would desire to have it searched to the bottom: who would not be content to have their souls searched, so they may have them saved?

II. The matter in the text

'The kingdom of heaven suffereth violence, and the violent take it by force.'

What is meant by the kingdom of heaven?

Some interpret it of the doctrine of the gospel, which reveals Christ and heaven. – So Erasmus.

But I rather by the kingdom of heaven understand, 'glory': and so learned Beza and others.

This kingdom 'suffereth violence.'

'Tis a metaphor from a town or castle that holds out in war, and is not taken but by storm. So the kingdom of heaven will not be taken without violence; 'the violent take it by force.'

The earth is inherited by the meek (Matt. 5:5), heaven is inherited by the violent. Our life is military, Christ is our captain, the gospel is the banner, the graces are our spiritual artillery, and heaven is only taken in a forcible way. The words fall into two parts:

1. The combat: 'suffereth violence.'
2. The conquest: the 'violent take it by force.'

Doctrine: *The right way to take heaven is by storm: or thus, none get into heaven but violent ones.*

This violence has a double aspect.

I. Application to magistrates

It concerns men *as magistrates;* they must be violent.

(1) *In punishing the nocent.*[1] When Aaron's Urim and Thummim will do no good, then must Moses come with his rod. The wicked are the bad humours and surfeit of the commonwealth, which by the care of magistracy are to be purged out. God hath placed governors 'for the terror of evildoers' (1 Pet. 2:14). They must not be like the swordfish, which hath a sword in his head, but is without a heart. They

---
[1] [The guilty.]

must not have a sword in their hand, but no heart to draw it out for the cutting down of impiety. Connivance in a magistrate supports vice, and by not punishing offenders he adopts other men's faults and makes them his own. Magistracy without zeal is like the body without the spirits. Too much lenity emboldens sin, and doth but shave the head which deserves to be cut off.

(2) *In defending the innocent.* The magistrate is the asylum or altar of refuge for the oppressed to fly to. Charles, duke of Calabria, was so in love with doing justice, that he caused a bell to be hung at his palace gate, which whosoever did ring was sure presently to be admitted into the duke's presence, or have some officers sent out to hear his cause. Aristides was famous for his justice, of whom the historian saith, he would never favour any man's cause because he was his friend, nor do injustice to any because he was his enemy. The magistrate's balance is the oppressed man's shield.

II. Application to Christians

This violence concerns men *as Christians*. Though heaven be given us freely, yet we must contend for it. 'What thy hand findeth to do, do it with all thy might' (Eccles. 9:10). Our work is great, our time short, our master urgent; we have need therefore to summon together all the powers of our souls, and strive as in a matter of life and death, that we may arrive at the kingdom above: we must not only put forth diligence, but violence. For the illustrating and clearing the proposition, I shall show,

1. *What violence is not meant here:* This violence in the text excludes:

(1) An *ignorant* violence; to be violent for that which we do not understand. 'As I passed by and beheld your devotions, I found an altar with this inscription, to the unknown God' (Acts 17:23). These Athenians were violent in their devotion; but it might be said to them, as Christ said to the woman of Samaria, 'Ye worship ye know not what' (John 4:22). Thus the Catholics are violent in their religion: witness their penance, fasting, dilacerating themselves till the blood comes, but it is a zeal without knowledge: their mettle is better than their eyesight. When Aaron was to burn the incense upon the altar, he was first to light the lamps (Exod. 25:7). When zeal like incense burns, first the lamp of knowledge must be lighted.

(2) It excludes a *bloody* violence, which is twofold:

First, *when one goes to lay violent hands upon himself*. The body is an earthly prison where God hath put the soul; we must not break prison, but stay till God by death lets us out. The sentinel is not to stir without leave from his captain, nor must we dare to stir hence without God's leave. Our bodies are the temples of the Holy Ghost (1 Cor. 6:19); when we offer violence to them, we destroy God's temple. The lamp of life must burn so long as any natural moisture is left like oil to feed it.

Secondly, *when one takes away the life of another*. There's too much of this violence nowadays. No sin hath a louder voice than blood: 'The voice of thy brother's blood crieth unto me from the ground' (Gen. 4:10). If there is a curse for him that 'smites his neighbour secretly' (Deut. 27:24), then he is double cursed that kills him. If a man had slain another unawares, he might take sanctuary and fly to the altar. But if he had done it willingly, the holiness of the place was not to protect him. 'If a man come presumptuously upon his neighbour to slay him with guile, thou shalt take him from mine altar that he may die' (Exod. 21:14). Joab being a man of blood, King Solomon sought to slay him, though he caught hold of the horns of the altar (1 Kings 2:28, 29). In Bohemia formerly, the murderer was to be beheaded and put in the same coffin with him whom he killed. Thus we see what violence the text excludes.

2. *What violence is meant here;* it is a *holy* violence. This is twofold.

(1) We must be violent *for the truth*. Here Pilate's question will be moved, 'What is truth?' Truth is either the blessed word of God, which is called the 'word of truth,' or those doctrinals which are deduced from the word and agree with it, as the dial with the sun or the transcript with the original – such as the doctrine of the Trinity, the doctrine of the creation, the doctrine of free grace, justification by the blood of Christ, regeneration, resurrection of the dead, and the life of glory. These truths we must be violent for, which is either by being advocates for them or martyrs.

Truth is the most glorious thing; the least filing of this gold is precious. What shall we be violent for, if not for truth? Truth is ancient, its grey hairs may make it venerable. It comes from him who is the Ancient of Days. Truth is unerring, it is the star which leads to Christ. Truth is pure (Psa. 119:140), it is compared to 'silver refined seven times' (Psa. 12:6). There is not the least spot on truth's face; it breathes nothing but sanctity. Truth is triumphant: it is like a great conqueror; when all its enemies lie dead, it keeps the field, and sets up its trophies of victory. Truth may be opposed, but never quite deposed. In the time of Diocletian, things seemed desperate, truth ran low; soon after was the golden time of Constantine, and then truth did again lift up its head. When the water in the Thames is lowest, a high tide is ready to come in. God is on truth's side, and so long there is no fear but it will prevail. 'The heavens being on fire shall be dissolved,' but not that truth which came from heaven (2 Pet. 3:12; 1 Pet. 1:25).

Truth hath noble effects. Truth is the seed of the new birth. God doth not regenerate us by miracles, or revelations, but by 'the word of truth' (James 1:18). As truth is the breeder of grace, so the feeder of it (1 Tim. 4:6). Truth sanctifies: 'Sanctify them by thy truth' (John 17:17). Truth is the seal that leaves the print of its own holiness upon us. It is both *speculum* and *lavacrum,* a *glass* to show us our blemishes, and a *laver* to wash them away. Truth 'makes us free' (John 8:32): it bears off the fetters of sin, and puts us into a state of sonship and 'kingship' (Rom. 8:14; Rev. 1:6). Truth is comforting: this wine cheers. When David's harp and viol could yield him no comfort, truth did: 'This is my comfort in my affliction, for thy word hath quickened me' (Psa. 119:50). Truth is an antidote against error. Error is the adultery of the mind: it stains the soul, as treason doth the blood. Error damns as well as vice. A man may as well die by poison as pistol. And what can stave off error but truth? The reason so many have been trappaned[1] into error is because they either did not know or did not love the truth. I can never say enough in the honour of truth. Truth is *basis fidei,* the ground of our faith; it gives us an exact model of religion; it shows us what we are to believe. Take away truth and our

---

[1] [Cheated or betrayed.]

faith is fancy. Truth is the best flower in the church's crown. We have not a richer jewel to trust God with than our souls, nor he a richer jewel to trust us with than his truths. Truth is *insigne honoris,* an ensign of honour. It distinguishes us from the false church, as chastity distinguisheth a virtuous woman from a harlot. In short, truth is *ecclesiae praesidium,* the bulwark of a nation: it is said the Levites (who were the antesignani, the ensign-bearers of truth) strengthened the kingdom (2 Chron. 11:17). Truth may be compared to the capitol of Rome, which was a place of the greatest strength; or the Tower of David, on which there hung a thousand shields (Song of Sol. 4:4). Our forts and navies do not so much strengthen us as truth. Truth is the best militia of a kingdom. If once we part with truth, and espouse popery, the lock is cut where our strength lies. What then should we be violent for, if not for truth? We are bid to contend as in an agony 'for the faith delivered to the saints' (Jude 3). If truth once be gone, we may write this epitaph on England's tombstone: 'Thy glory is departed.'

(2) This holy violence is when we are violent for our own salvation. 'Give all diligence to make your calling and election sure' (2 Pet. 1:10). The Greek word signifies *anxious carefulness,* or a serious bearing one's thoughts about the business of eternity; such a care as sets head and heart at work. In this channel of religion all a Christian's zeal should run.

3. *The third thing is, what is implied in this holy violence?* It implies three things: (1) Resolution of will; (2) Vigour of affection; (3) Strength of endeavour.

(1) *Resolution of the will.* 'I have sworn and will perform it, that I will keep thy righteous judgments' (Psa. 119:106). Whatever is in the way to heaven (though there be a lion

in the way), I will encounter it. Like a resolute commander that chargeth through the whole body of the army. The Christian is resolved, come what may, he will have heaven. Where there is this resolution, danger must be despised, difficulties trampled upon, terrors contemned. This is the first thing in holy violence, resolution of will – I will have heaven whatever it costs me – and this resolution must be in the strength of Christ.

Resolution is like the bias to the bowl, which carries it strongly. Where there is but half a resolution, a will to be saved and a will to follow sin, it is impossible to be violent for heaven. If a traveller be unresolved, sometimes he will ride this way, sometimes that; he is violent for neither.

(2) *Vigour of the affections.* The will proceeds upon reason: the judgment being informed of the excellency of a state of glory, and the will being resolved upon a voyage to that holy land, now the affections follow, and they are on fire in passionate longings after heaven. The affections are violent things: 'My soul thirsteth for God, for the living God' (Psa. 42:2). The Rabbis note here that David saith not, My soul 'hungereth,' but 'thirsteth,' because naturally we are more impatient of thirst than hunger. See in what a rapid violent motion David's affections were carried after God. The affections are like the wings of the bird, which make the soul swift in its flight after glory. Where the affections are stirred up, there is offering violence to heaven.

(3) This violence implies *strength of endeavour,* when we strive for salvation as about a matter of life and death. It is easy to talk of heaven, but not to get to heaven; we must *operam navare,* put forth all our strength; nay, call in the help of heaven to this work.

4. *The fourth thing is, how many ways a Christian must offer violence?* Four ways: he must offer violence:

    I. To Himself;
    II. To Satan;
    III. To the World;
    IV. To Heaven.

I. He Must Offer Violence to Himself

This self-violence consists in two things: 1. Mortification of sin; 2. Provocation to duty.

1. Mortification of sin

Offering violence to one's self in a spiritual sense, consists in *mortification of sin*. 'Self' is the 'flesh'; this we must offer violence to. Jerome, Chrysostom, Theophylact do all expound 'taking heaven by force,' as 'the mortifying the flesh' (Rom. 8:13). The flesh is a bosom-traitor. It is like the Trojan horse within the walls, which doth all the mischief. The flesh is a sly enemy; at first it is *dulce venenum*,[1] afterwards *scorpio pungens*.[2] It kills by embracing. The embraces of the flesh are like the ivy embracing the oak which sucks out the strength fit for its own leaves and berries: so the flesh by its soft embraces sucks out all heart for good. 'The flesh lusteth against the spirit' (Gal. 5:17). The pampering of the flesh is the quenching of God's Spirit. The flesh chokes and stifles holy motions. The flesh sides with Satan, and is true to his interest. There is a party within that will not pray, that will not believe. The flesh inclines us more to believe a temptation than a promise. There needs no wind to blow

[1] [A sweet poison.]
[2] [A stinging scorpion.]

to sin, when this tide within is so strong to carry us thither. The flesh being so near to us, its counsels are more attractive. No chain of adamant binds so fast as the chain of lust. Alexander, who was *victor mundi,* conqueror of the world, was *captivus viliorum,* led captive by vice.

Now a man must offer violence to his fleshly desires if he will be saved. 'Mortify therefore your members which are upon the earth' (Col. 3:5). The mortifying and killing of sin at the root is when we not only forbear the acts of sin, but hate the inbeing. *Plurimi peccata radunt non eradicant*[1] (Bernard).

Nay, where sin hath received its deadly wound, and is in part abated, yet the work of mortification is not to be laid aside. The apostle persuades the believing Romans to 'mortify the deeds of the flesh' (Rom. 8:13). In the best of saints there is something that needs mortifying; much pride, envy, passion; therefore mortification is called crucifixion (Gal. 5:24), which is not done suddenly: every day some limb of the 'body of death' must drop off. Nothing harder than a rock, saith Cyril, yet in the clefts thereof some weed or other will fasten its roots: none stronger than a believer, yet do what he can, sin will fasten its roots in him, and spring out sometimes by inordinate desires. There is something that needs mortifying. Hence it was St Paul did 'beat down his body,' by prayer, watching, fasting (1 Cor. 9:27).

But, is it not said, 'no man ever hated his own flesh?' (Eph. 5:29).

---

[1] [Most people brush over their sins rather than uproot them.]

As flesh is taken physically for the bodily compages[1] or constitution, so it is to be cherished; but as flesh is taken theologically for the impure lustings of the flesh, so a man must hate his own flesh. The apostle saith, 'Fleshly lusts war against the soul' (1 Pet. 2:11). If the flesh doth war against us, there is good reason we should war against the flesh.

How may one do to offer violence to himself in mortifying the flesh?

First, Withdraw the fuel that may make lust burn. Avoid all temptations. Take heed of that which doth nourish sin. He that would suppress the gout or stone, avoids those foods which are noxious. They who pray they may not be led into temptation, must not lead themselves into temptation.

Second, Fight against fleshly lusts with spiritual weapons; faith and prayer. The best way to combat with sin is upon our knees. Run to the promise, 'Sin shall not have dominion over you' (Rom. 6:14); or as the Greek word is, it shall not lord it. Beg strength of Christ (Phil. 4:13). Samson's strength lay in his hair, ours lies in our Head, Christ. This is one way of offering violence to one's self by mortification. This is a mystery to the major part of the world, who do rather gratify the flesh than mortify it.

2. Provocation to duty

The second thing wherein offering violence to a man's self consists is in *provocation to duty*. Then we offer holy violence to ourselves when we excite and provoke ourselves to that which is good. This is called in Scripture a 'stirring up ourselves to take hold of God' (Isa. 64:7) Consider,

---

[1] [Structure.]

(1) *What absolute need there is to stir up ourselves to holy duties.* In respect of the sluggishness of our hearts to that which is spiritual: blunt tools need whetting, a dull creature needs spurs. Our hearts are dull and heavy in the things of God, therefore we had need to spur them on, and provoke them to that which is good. The flesh hinders from duty. When we would pray, the flesh resists; when we should suffer, the flesh draws back. How hard is it sometimes to get leave of our hearts to seek God! Jesus Christ went more willingly to the cross, than we do to the throne of grace. Had not we need then provoke ourselves to duty? If our hearts are so unstrung in religion, we had need prepare and put them in tune.

The exercises of God's worship are contrary to nature; therefore there must be a provoking of ourselves to them. The motion of the soul to sin is natural, but its motion towards heaven is violent. The stone moves easily to the centre; it hath an innate propensity downward; but to draw up a millstone into the air is done by violence, because it is against nature: so to lift up the heart to heaven in duty, is done by violence, and we must provoke ourselves to it.

(2) *What it is to provoke ourselves to duty.*

(i) *It is to awaken ourselves and shake off spiritual sloth.* Holy David awakens his tongue and heart when he went about God's service, 'Awake up my glory, I myself will awaken early' (Psa. 57:8). He found a somnolency[1] and dullness in his soul; therefore did he provoke himself to duty: 'I myself will awake early.' Christians, though they are raised from the death of sin, yet often they fall asleep.

---

[1] [Sleepiness.]

(ii) *Provoking ourselves to duty, implies a uniting, and rallying together all the powers of our soul, and setting them on work in the exercises of religion.* A man saith to his thoughts, 'Be fixed on God in this duty'; and to his affections, 'Serve the Lord without distraction.' Matters of religion are done with intenseness of spirit.

(3) The third thing is to show *the several duties of Christianity,* wherein we must provoke and offer violence to ourselves. I shall name seven.

1st. *We must provoke ourselves to reading of the word.* What an infinite mercy is it that God hath honoured us with the Scriptures! The barbarous Indians have not the oracles of God made known to them. They have the golden mines, but not the Scriptures, which are more to be desired 'than much fine gold' (Psa. 19:10). Our Saviour bids us 'search the Scriptures' (John 5:39). We must not read these holy lines carelessly, as if they did not concern us, or run them over hastily, as Israel did eat the passover in haste; but peruse them with reverence and seriousness. The noble Bereans did 'search the Scriptures daily' (Acts 17:11). The Scripture is the pandect[1] of divine knowledge; it is the rule and touchstone of truth; out of this well we draw the water of life.

To provoke to a diligent reading of the word, labour to have a right notion of Scripture.

Read the word as a book made by God himself. It is given 'by divine inspiration' (2 Tim. 3:16). It is the library of the Holy Ghost. The prophets and apostles were but God's amanuenses or notaries to write the law at his mouth. The word is of divine original, and reveals the deep things of

---

[1] [A treatise or book that covers the whole of any subject.]

God to us. That there is a numen or deity is engraven in man's heart, and is to be read in the book of the creatures;

quaelibet herba Deum;[1]

but who this God is, and the Trinity of persons in the Godhead, is infinitely above the light of reason: only God himself could make this known. So also for the incarnation of Christ, God and man hypostatically united in one person; the mystery of imputed righteousness; the doctrine of faith: what angel in heaven, who but God himself, could reveal these things to us? How may this provoke to diligence and seriousness in reading the word which is divinely inspired. Other books may be made by holy men, but this book is indicted by the Holy Ghost.

Read the word as a perfect rule of faith. It contains all things essential to salvation. 'I adore the fulness of Scripture,' saith Tertullian. The word teacheth us how to please God, how to order our conversation in the world. It instructs us in all things that belong either to prudence or piety. How we should read the word with care and reverence, when it contains a perfect model and platform of religion, and is able to 'make us wise to salvation' (2 Tim. 3:15)!

When you read the word, look on it as a soul-enriching treasury. Search here as for a 'vein of silver' (Prov. 2:4). In this word are scattered many divine aphorisms; gather them up as so many jewels. This blessed book helps to enrich you; it fills your head with knowledge, and your heart with grace; it stores you with promises: a man may

---

[1] [*Praesentem monstrat quaelibet herba deum* = 'Every herb points out the presence of God.' The quotation is from the German poet Johannes Stigelius (1515–62).]

be rich in bonds. In this field the pearl of price is his. What are all the world's riches to these? Islands of spices, coasts of pearl, rocks of diamonds! These are but the riches that reprobates may have, but the word gives us those riches which angels have.

Read the word as a book of evidences. How carefully doth one read over his evidences! Would you know whether God be your God? Search the records of Scripture: 'Hereby we know he abides in us, by the Spirit which he hath given us' (1 John 3:24). Would you know whether you are heirs of the promise? You must find it in these sacred writings: 'He hath chosen us to salvation through sanctification' (2 Thess. 2:13). They who are vessels of grace, shall be vessels of glory.

Look upon the word as a spiritual magazine out of which you fetch all your weapons to fight against sin and Satan. (i) Here are weapons to *fight against sin*. The word of God is a consecrated sword that cuts asunder the lusts of the heart. When pride begins to lift up itself, the sword of the Spirit destroys this sin: 'God resists the proud' (1 Pet. 5:5). When passion vents itself, the word of God, like Hercules' club, beats down this angry fury: 'Anger rests in the bosom of fools' (Eccles. 7:9). When lust boils, the word of God cools that intemperate heat: 'No unclean person hath any inheritance in the kingdom of Christ' (Eph. 5:5). (ii) Here are weapons to *fight against Satan*. The word fenceth off temptation. When the devil tempted Christ, he three times wounded the old Serpent with the sword of the Spirit: 'It is written' (Matt. 4:7). Satan never sooner foils a Christian than when he is unarmed, and without scripture weapons.

Look upon the word as a spiritual glass to dress yourselves by. It is a looking-glass for the blind (Psa. 19:8). In other

[17]

glasses you may see your faces; in this glass you may see your hearts: 'Through thy precepts I get understanding' (Psa. 119:104). This looking-glass of the word clearly represents Christ: it sets him forth in his person, nature, offices, as most precious and eligible: 'He is altogether lovely' (Song of Sol. 5:16). He is a wonder of beauty, a paradise of delight. Christ who was veiled over in types is clearly revealed in the glass of the Scriptures.

Look upon the word as a book of spiritual receipts. Basil compares the word to an apothecary's shop, which hath all kind of medicines and antidotes. If you find yourselves dead in duty, here is a receipt: 'Thy word hath quickened me' (Psa. 119:50). If you find your hearts hard, the word doth liquify and melt them. Therefore it is compared to fire for its mollifying power (Jer. 23:29). If you are poisoned with sin, here is a herb to expel it.

Look upon the word as a sovereign elixir to comfort you in distress. It comforts you against all your sins, temptations, and afflictions. What are the promises, but divine cordials to revive fainting souls. A gracious heart goes feeding on a promise as Samson on the honeycomb (Judg. 14:9). The word comforts against sickness and death: 'O death, where is thy sting?' (1 Cor. 15:55). A Christian dies embracing the promise, as Simeon did Christ (Heb. 11:16).

Read the word as the last will and testament of Christ. Here are many legacies given to them that love him: pardon of sin, adoption, consolation. This will is in force, being sealed in Christ's blood. With what seriousness doth a child read over the will and testament of his father, that he may see what is left him!

Read it as a book by which you must be judged. 'The

OR, THE CHRISTIAN SOLDIER

word I have spoken shall judge him at the last day' (John 12:48). They who live according to the rules of this book shall be acquitted; they who live contrary to them shall be condemned. There are two books God will go by, the Book of Conscience, and the Book of Scripture: the one shall be the witness, and the other the judge. How should every Christian then provoke himself to read this book of God with care and devotion! This is that book which God will proceed by at the last. They who fly from the word as a guide, shall be forced to submit to it as a judge.

2nd. *We must provoke ourselves in hearing of the word.* We may bring our bodies to the word with ease, but not our hearts without offering violence to ourselves. When we come to the word preached, we come about a business of the highest importance; therefore we should stir up ourselves and hear with the greatest devotion. Constantine the emperor was noted for his reverend attention to the word. 'All the people were attentive to hear him' (Luke 19:48). In the Greek it is *they hanged upon his lip*. When the word is dispensed, we are now to lift up the everlasting doors of our hearts, that the King of glory may enter in.

[1] How far are they from offering violence to themselves in hearing *who scarce mind what is said, as if they were not at all concerned in the business.* They come to church more for custom than conscience. 'They come to thee as the people cometh, and they sit before thee as my people, and hear thy words, but they will not do them' (Ezek. 33:31). If we could tell them of a rich purchase, or of some place of preferment, they would diligently attend: but when the word of life is preached, they disregard it.

[2] How far are they from offering violence to themselves

HEAVEN TAKEN BY STORM

in hearing, *who come to the word in a dull, drowsy manner,* as if they came to church to take a receipt to make them sleep. The word is to feed; it is strange to sleep at meat. The word judgeth men; it is strange for a prisoner to fall asleep at the bar. To such sleepy hearers God may say, 'Sleep on.' He may suffer them to be so stupefied, that no ordinance shall awaken them: 'While men slept, the enemy came and sowed tares' (Matt. 13:25). The devil is never asleep, but sows the tares of sin in a drowsy hearer.

That we may when we come to the word offer violence to ourselves, and stir up ourselves to hear with devotion, consider,

[i] *It is God that speaks to us.* If a judge gives a charge upon the bench, all listen. If a king speaks, all give attention. When we come to the word, we should think thus with ourselves: We are to hear God in this preacher. Therefore Christ is said now to speak to us from heaven (Heb. 12:25). Christ speaks in his ministers, as a king speaketh in the person of his ambassador. When Samuel knew it was the Lord that spake to him, he lent an ear: 'Speak Lord, thy servant heareth' (1 Sam. 3:10). They who slight God speaking in his word, shall hear him speaking in his wrath: 'Then shall he speak to them in his wrath' (Psa. 2:5).

[ii] Let us consider *the weightiness of the matters delivered to us.* As Moses said to Israel, 'I call heaven and earth to record this day, that I have set before you life and death' (Deut. 30:19). We preach to men of Christ, and the eternal recompenses. Here are the *magnalia legis,* the weighty matters of the law; and doth not all this call for serious attention? There is a great deal of difference between a letter of news read to us, and a letter of special business wherein our

whole land and estate is concerned. In the word preached our salvation is concerned; here we are instructed to the kingdom of God, and if ever we will be serious, it should be now: 'It is not a vain thing for you because it is your life' (Deut. 32:47).

[iii] *If the word be not regarded, it will not be remembered.* Many complain they cannot remember – here is the reason: God punisheth their carelessness in hearing, with forgetfulness. He suffers Satan to take away the word from them: 'The fowls of the air came and devoured the seed' (Matt. 13:4). The devil is no recusant, he comes to church; but it is not for any good intent: he gets away the word from men. How many have been robbed of the sermon and their souls both at once.

[iv] *It may be the last time that ever God will speak to us in his word.* It may be the last sermon that ever we shall hear, and we may go from the place of hearing to the place of judging. Did people think thus when they come into the house of God: Perhaps this will be the last time that God will counsel us about our souls; the last time that ever we shall see our minister's face; with what devotion would they come! How would their affections be all on fire in hearing! We give great attention to the last speeches of friends; a parent's dying words are received as oracles. Oh let all this provoke us to diligence in hearing! Let us think this may be the last time that Aaron's bell shall sound in our ears, and before another day, we shall be in another world.

3rd. *The next way we are to offer violence to ourselves, is in prayer.* Prayer is a duty which keeps the trade of religion a-going. When we either join in prayer with others, or pray alone, we must use holy violence. Not eloquence in prayer, but violence carries it. Theodorus said, speaking of Luther, 'Once I overheard him in prayer; but (good God), with what life and spirit did he pray! It was with so much reverence as if he were speaking to God, yet with so much confidence, as if he had been speaking to his friend.' There must be a stirring up of the heart, [1] To prayer. [2] In prayer.

[1] A stirring up of the heart *to prayer,* 'If thou prepare thine heart, and stretch out thine hands towards him' (Job 11:13). This preparing of our heart is by holy thoughts and ejaculations. The musician first tunes his instrument before he plays.

[2] There must be a stirring up of the heart *in prayer.* Prayer is a lifting up of the mind and soul to God, which cannot be done aright without offering violence to oneself. The names given to prayer import violence. It is called 'wrestling' (Gen. 32:24), and 'pouring out the soul' (1 Sam. 1:15), both which imply vehemency. The affection is required as well as the invention. The apostle speaks of an 'effectual fervent prayer,' which is a parallel phrase to 'offering violence.'

Alas, how far are they from offering violence to themselves in prayer, that give God a *dead, heartless prayer!* God would not have the blind offered (Mal. 1:8); as good to offer the blind as the dead. Some are half asleep when they pray. And will a sleepy prayer ever awaken God? Such as mind not their own prayers, how do they think that God should mind them? Those prayers God likes best which come seething hot from the heart.

How far are they from offering violence that give God *distracted prayer!* While they are praying they are thinking of their shop and trade. How can he shoot right whose eye

OR, THE CHRISTIAN SOLDIER

is quite off the mark? 'Their heart goes after their covetousness' (Ezek. 33:31). Many are casting up their accounts in prayer, as Jerome once complained of himself. How can God be pleased with this? Will a king endure that while his subject is delivering a petition and speaking to him, he should be playing with a feather? When we send our hearts on an errand to heaven, how often do they loiter and play by the way? This is matter of blushing.

That we may offer violence to ourselves, and by fervency feather the wing of prayer, let these ten things be duly weighed: –

[i] *The majesty of God with whom we have to do*. He sees how it is with us in prayer, whether we are deeply affected with those things we pray for. 'The king came in to see the guests' (Matt. 22:11). So when we go to pray, the King of glory comes in to see in what frame we are; he hath a window which looks into our breasts, and if he sees a dead heart he may turn a deaf ear. Nothing will sooner make God's anger wax hot than a cold prayer.

[ii] *Prayer without fervency and violence, is no prayer;* it is speaking not praying. Lifeless prayer is no more prayer than the picture of a man is a man. To say a prayer is not to pray; Aschanius taught his parrot the Lord's Prayer. St Ambrose saith well, 'It is the life and affection in a duty that baptizeth it, and gives it a name.' It is the violence and wrestling of the affections that make it a prayer, else it is no prayer; but a man may say as Pharaoh, 'I have dreamed a dream' (Gen. 41:15).

[iii] *The zeal and violence of the affections in prayer best suits with God's nature*. He 'is a spirit' (John 4:24), and sure that prayer which is full of life and spirit is the savoury meat

[23]

he loves, 'spiritual sacrifices acceptable to God' (1 Pet. 2:5). Spirituality and fervency in duty are like the spirits of wine, which are the more refined part of the wine. Bodily exercise profits nothing. It is not the stretching of the lungs, but the vehemency of the desire that makes music in God's ears.

[iv] *Consider the need we have of those things which we ask in prayer.* We come to ask the favour of God; and if we have not his love, all that we enjoy is cursed to us. We pray that our souls may be washed in Christ's blood; and if he wash us not, 'we have no part in him.' These are such mercies, that if God deny us, we are forever undone. Therefore what violence had we need put forth in prayer? When will a man be earnest, if not when he is begging for his life?

[v] *Let it provoke violence in prayer to consider those things which we ask, God hath a mind to grant.* If a son ask nothing but what his father is willing to bestow, he may be the more earnest in his suit. We go to God for pardon of sin, and no work more pleasing to him than to seal pardons. Mercy is his delight (Mic. 7:18). We pray to God for a holy heart, and this prayer is according to his will, 'This is the will of God, your sanctification' (1 Thess. 4:3). We pray that God would give us a heart to love him. How pleasing must this request needs be to God! This, if anything may excite prayer, and carry in it a fiery chariot up to heaven, when we know we pray for nothing but what God is more willing to grant than we are to ask.

[vi] *No mercy can be bestowed on us but in a way of prayer.* Mercy is purchased by Christ's blood, but it is conveyed by prayer. All the promises are bonds made over to us, but prayer puts these bonds in suit. The Lord hath told Israel with what rich mercy he would bespangle them;

he would bring them to their native country, and bring them thither with 'new hearts' (Ezek. 36:26). Yet this tree of the promise would not drop its fruit till shaken with the hand of prayer. For 'all this will I yet be enquired' (Ezek. 36:37). The breast of God's mercy is full, but prayer must draw the breast. Surely, if all other ways are blocked up, there's no good to be done without prayer. How should we ply this oar, and by a holy violence stir up ourselves to take hold of God!

[vii] *It is only violence and intenseness of spirit in prayer that hath the promise of mercy affixed to it:* '*Knock and it shall be opened*' (Matt. 7:7). Knocking is a violent motion. The Aediles[1] among the Romans had their doors always standing open, that all who had petitions might have free access to them. God's heart is ever open to fervent prayer. Let us then be fired with zeal, and with Christ pray yet more earnestly (Luke 22:44). It is violence in prayer that makes heaven's gates fly open, and fetcheth in whatever mercies we stand in need of.

[viii] *The large returns God hath given to violent prayer.* This dove sent to heaven, hath often brought an olive leaf in its mouth, 'This poor man cried, and the Lord heard him' (Psa. 34:6). 'Crying' prayer prevails. Daniel in the den prayed and prevailed. Prayer did shut the lion's mouth and open the lion's den. Fervent prayer, saith one, hath a kind of omnipotency in it. Sozomen saith of Apollonius, that he never asked anything of God in all his life that he obtained not. Sleidan reports of Luther, that perceiving the interest of religion to be low, he betook himself to prayer; at length rising off his knees, he came out of his closet triumphantly,

---

[1] [Local government officials in ancient Rome.]

saying to his friends, '*Vicimus, Vicimus,*' 'We have overcome, we have overcome.' At which time, it was observed, there came out a proclamation from Charles V, that none should be further molested for the profession of the gospel. How may this encourage us, and make us hoist up the sails of prayer, when others of the saints have had such good returns from the holy land!

That we may put forth this holy violence in prayer, it is requisite there be a renewed principle of grace. If the person be graceless, no wonder the prayer is heartless. The body while it is dead hath no heat in it: while a man is dead in sin, he can have no heat in duty.

[ix] *That we may be the more violent in prayer, it is good to pray with a sense of our wants.* A beggar that is pinched with want, will be earnest in craving an alms. Christian, review thy wants: thou wantest an humble spiritual frame of heart; thou wantest the light of God's countenance: the sense of want will quicken prayer. That man can never pray fervently that doth not pray feelingly. How earnest was Samson for water when he was ready to die: 'I die for thirst' (Judg. 15:18).

[x] *If we would be violent in prayer, let us beg a violent wind.* The Spirit of God is resembled to 'a mighty rushing wind' (Acts 2:2). Then we are violent, when this blessed wind fills our sails, Jude 20: 'Praying in the Holy Ghost.' If any fire be in our sacrifice, it comes down from heaven.

4th. *The next duty wherein we must offer violence to ourselves, is meditation;* a duty wherein the very heart and life-blood of religion lies.

St Bernard calls meditation *animae viaticum,* a bait by the way. Meditation may be thus described; it is a holy exercise of the mind, whereby we bring the truths of God to remembrance, and do seriously ponder upon them, and apply them to ourselves.

In meditation there are two things: [1] *A Christian's retiring of himself, a locking himself up from the world.* Meditation is a work which cannot be done in a crowd. [2] *It is a serious thinking on God.* It is not a few transient thoughts that are quickly gone, but a fixing and staying the mind upon heavenly objects. This cannot be done without exciting all the powers of our souls, and offering violence to ourselves.

We are the more to provoke ourselves to this duty, because, [1] *Meditation is so cross to flesh and blood.* Naturally we shun holy meditation. To meditate on worldly secular things, if it were all day, we can do it without any diversion. But to have our thoughts fixed on God, how hard do we find it! How do our hearts quarrel with this duty! What pleas and excuses have we to shift it off! The natural averseness from this duty shows we are to offer violence to ourselves in it. [2] *Satan doth what he can to hinder this duty.* He is an enemy to meditation. The devil cares not how much we hear, nor how little we meditate. Hearing begets knowledge, but meditation begets devotion. Meditation doth ballast the heart, and make it serious; and Satan labours to keep the heart from being serious. What need therefore is there of offering violence to ourselves in this duty!

But methinks I hear some say, when they sit alone they know not what to meditate of; I shall therefore furnish them with *matter* of meditation.

[1] *Meditate seriously upon the corruption of your nature.* We have lost that pure quintessential frame of soul that

once we had. There is a sea of sin in us. Our nature is a source and seminary of all evil, like Peter's sheet, wherein were 'wild beasts and creeping things' (Acts 10:12). This sin cleaves to us as a leprosy. This original pollution makes us guilty before the Lord; and though we should never commit actual sin, this merits hell. The meditation of this would be a means to pull down our pride. Nay, even those that have grace have cause to walk humbly, because they have more corruption in them than grace: their dark side is broader than their light.

[2] *Meditate seriously upon the death and passion of Christ.* His soul was overcast with a cloud of sorrow when he was conflicting with his Father's wrath; and all this we should have suffered. 'He was wounded for our transgressions' (Isa. 53:5). As David said, 'Lo I have sinned, but these sheep, what have they done?' (2 Sam. 24:17). So we have sinned, but this Lamb of God, what had he done?

[i] The serious meditation of this would *produce repentance*. How could we look upon him 'whom we have pierced' (Zech. 12:10; John 19:37) and not mourn over him? When we consider how dear our sins cost Christ, how should we shed the blood of our sins which shed Christ's blood!

[ii] The meditation of Christ's death would *fire our hearts with love to Christ*. What friend shall we love, if not him who died for us? His love to us made him cruel to himself. As Rebecca said to Jacob, 'Upon me be thy curse' (Gen. 27:13); so said Christ, 'Upon me be thy curse,' that poor sinners may inherit the blessing.

[3] *Meditate on your evidences for heaven.* What have you to show for heaven, if you should die this night?

[i] *Was your heart ever thoroughly convinced of sin?* Did

you ever see yourself lost without Christ? Conviction is the first step to conversion (John 16:7:11).

[ii] *Hath God ever made you willing to take Christ upon his own terms?* 'He shall be a priest upon his throne' (Zech. 6:13). Are you as willing that Christ should be upon the throne of your heart to rule, as a friend at the altar to intercede? Are you willing to renounce those sins to which the bias of your heart doth naturally incline? Can you set those sins as Uriah in the forefront of the battle to be slain? Are you willing to take Christ for better for worse; to take him with his cross, and to avouch Christ in the worst of times?

[iii] *Have you the indwelling presence of the Spirit?* If you have, what hath God's Spirit done in you? Hath it made you of another spirit: meek, merciful, humble? Is it a transforming Spirit? Hath it left the impression of its own holiness upon you? These are good evidences for heaven. By these, as by a spiritual touchstone, you may know whether you have grace or not. Beware of false evidences. None are further from having the true pearl, than they that content themselves with the counterfeit.

[4] *Meditate upon the uncertainty of all sublunary comforts.* Creature-delights have their flux and reflux. How oft doth the sun of worldly pomp and grandeur go down at noon. Xerxes was forced to fly away in a small vessel, who but a little before wanted sea-room for his navy. We say everything is mutable, but who meditates upon it? The world is resembled to a 'sea of glass mingled with fire' (Rev. 15:2). Glass is slippery, it hath no sure footing; and glass mingled with fire is subject to consume. All creatures are fluid and uncertain, and cannot be made to fix. What is become of the glory of Athens, the pomp of Troy? 'The

world passeth away' (1 John 2:17). It slides away as a ship in full sail. How quickly doth the scene alter, and a low ebb succeed a high tide? There's no trusting to anything. Health may be turned to sickness, friends may die, riches may take wings. We are ever upon the tropics. The serious meditation of this would:

[i] *Keep us from being so deceived by the world.* We are ready to set up our rest here: 'Their inward thought is that their houses shall continue for ever' (Psa. 49:11). We are apt to think that our mountain stands strong (Psa. 30:7). We dream of an earthly eternity. Alas, did we meditate how casual and uncertain these things are, we should not be so often deluded. Have not we seen great disappointments, and where we have thought to suck honey, there we have drank wormwood?

[ii] The meditation of the uncertainty of all things under the sun, *would much moderate our affections to them.* Why should we so eagerly pursue an uncertainty? Many take care to get a great estate; it is uncertain whether they shall keep it. The fire may break in where the thief cannot. Or if they do keep it, it is a question whether they shall have the comfort of it. They lay up for a child; that child may die; or if he live, he may prove a burden. This seriously meditated on would cure the dropsy of covetousness, and make us sit loose to that which hangs so loose, and is ready to drop off from us.

[iii] The meditation of this uncertainty *would make us look after a certainty; that is, the getting of grace.* This holy 'anointing abides' (1 John 2:27). Grace is a flower of eternity.

Non fertur ad umbras inclyta virtus.[1]

Death does not destroy grace, but transplants it and makes it grow in a better soil. He that hath true holiness can no more lose it than the angels can which are fixed stars in glory.

[5] *Meditate of God's severity against sin.* Every arrow in God's quiver is shot against it. Sin burned Sodom and drowned the old world. Sin kindles hell. If when a spark of God's wrath flies into a man's conscience, it is so terrible: what is it then, when God 'stirs up all his wrath' (Psa. 78:38)! The meditation of this would frighten us out of our sins. There cannot be so much sweetness in sin as there is sting. How dreadful is God's anger! 'Who knoweth the power of his wrath?' (Psa. 90:11). All fire, compared with the fire of God's wrath, is painted and imaginary. Oh that every time we meddle with sin, we would think with ourselves we choose the bramble, and fire will come out of this bramble to devour us.

[6] *Meditate on eternal life,* 'This is his promise, even eternal life' (1 John 2:25). Life is sweet, and this word 'eternal' makes it sweeter. This lies in the immediate vision and fruition of God. [i] This is a *spiritual* life: it is opposite to that animal life which we live now. Here we hunger and thirst; but there we shall 'hunger no more' (Rev. 7:16). There is the marriage supper of the Lamb, which will not only satisfy hunger, but prevent it. That blessed life to come doth not consist in sensual delights, meat and drink, and music; nor in the comfort of relations; but the soul will be wholly swallowed up in God, and acquiesce in him with infinite

---

[1] [Celebrated virtue is not carried off with death.]

complacency. As when the sun appears, the stars vanish; so when God shall appear in his glory, and fill the soul, then all earthly sensitive delights shall vanish. [ii] It is a *glorious* life. The bodies of the saints shall be enamelled with glory: they shall be made like Christ's glorious body (Phil. 3:21). And if the cabinet be of such curious needlework, how rich shall the jewel be that is put into it! How bespangled with glory shall the soul be! Every saint shall wear his white robe, and have his throne to sit upon. Then God will put some of his own glory upon the saints. Glory shall not only be revealed to them, but in them (Rom. 8:18) And this life of glory shall be crowned with eternity; what angel can express it! Oh let us often meditate on this.

The meditation of eternal life would make us labour for a spiritual life. The child must be born before it is crowned. We must be born of the spirit, before we are crowned with glory.

The meditation of eternal life would comfort us in regard of the shortness of natural life. Our life we live now, flies away as a shadow: it is called 'a flower' (Psa. 103:15) 'a vapour' (James 4:14). Job sets forth fragile life very elegantly in three of the elements: land, water, air (Job 9:25, 26). Go to the land, and there man's life is like a swift post. Go to the water, there man's life is like a ship under sail. Look to the air, and there man's life is like a flying eagle. We are hastening to the grave. When our years do increase, our life doth decrease. Death creeps upon us by degrees. When our sight grows dim, there death creeps in at the eye. When our hearing is bad, there death creeps in at the ear. When our legs tremble under us, there is death pulling down the main pillars of the house; but eternal life comforts us against the shortness of natural life. That life to come is subject to no infirmities; it knows no period; we shall be 'as the angels of God,' capable of no mutation or change.

Thus you have seen six noble subjects for your thoughts to expatiate upon.

But where is the meditating Christian? Here I might lament the want of holy meditation. Most people live in a hurry. They are so distracted with the cares of the world, that they can find no time to meditate, or scarce ask their souls how they do. We are not like the saints in former ages. David did meditate in God's precepts (Psa. 119:15). 'Isaac walked in the evening to meditate' (Gen. 24:63). He did take a turn with God. What devout meditations do we read in St Augustine and Anselm! But it is too much out of date among our modern Christians.

Terra Astraea reliquit.[1]

Those beasts under the law which did not chew the cud, were unclean. Such as do not chew the cud by holy meditation are to be reckoned among the unclean. But I shall rather turn my lamentation into a persuasion, entreating Christians to offer violence to themselves in this so necessary duty of meditation. Pythagoras sequestered himself from all society, and lived in a cave for a whole year, that he might meditate upon philosophy. How then should we retire and lock up ourselves at least once a day, that we may meditate upon glory!

[1] *Meditation makes the word preached to profit;* it works it upon the consciences. As the bee sucks the flower,

---

[1] [The golden age has ended; lit. 'When Justice forsakes the earth and joins the stars' (Ovid).]

so by meditation we suck out the sweetness of a truth. It is not the receiving of meat into the mouth, but the digesting of it makes it nutritive. So it is not the receiving the most excellent truths in at the ear, that nourisheth our souls, but the digesting them by meditation. Wine poured in a sieve runs out. Many truths are lost, because ministers pour their wine into sieves, either into leaking memories or feathery minds. Meditation is like a soaking rain, that goes to the root of a tree, and makes it bring forth fruit.

[2] *Holy meditation quickens the affections.* 'O how love I thy law! it is my meditation all the day' (Psa. 119:97). The reason our affections are so cold to heavenly things, is because we do not warm them at the fire of holy meditation. As the musing on amorous objects makes the fire of lust burn, the musing on injuries makes the fire of revenge burn, so meditating on the transcendent beauties of Christ, would make our love to Christ flame forth.

[3] *Meditation hath a transforming power in it.* The hearing of the word may affect us; but the meditating of it doth transform us. Meditation stamps the impression of divine truths upon our hearts. By meditating of God's holiness, we grow holy. As Jacob's cattle by looking on the rods, conceived like the rods: so while by meditation we look upon God's purity, we are changed into his likeness, and are made partakers of his divine nature.

[4] *Meditation produceth reformation,* 'I thought on my ways, and turned my feet unto thy testimonies' (Psa. 119:59). Did but people meditate on the damnableness of sin, did they but think when they meddle with it, there is a rope at the end of it which will hang them eternally in hell, they would break off a course of sinning and become new creatures.

Let all this persuade to holy meditation. I dare be bold to say, if men would spend but one quarter of an hour every day in contemplating heavenly objects, it would leave a mighty impression upon them, and through the blessing of God, might prove the beginning of a happy conversion.

But how shall we do to meditate? Get a love to spiritual things. We usually meditate on those things which we love. The voluptuous man can muse on his pleasures, the covetous man on his bags of gold. Did we love heavenly things, we should meditate more on them. Many say they cannot meditate because they want[1] memory; but is it not rather because they want affection? Did they love the things of God, they would make them their continual study and meditation.

5th. *The next duty wherein we are to offer violence to ourselves, is self-examination;* a duty of great importance: it is a parleying with one's own heart, 'I commune with my own heart' (Psa. 77:6).

David did put interrogatories to himself. Self-examination is the setting up a court in conscience, and keeping a register there, that by strict scrutiny a man may know how things stand between God and his own soul. Self-examination is a spiritual inquisition, a bringing of oneself to trial. A good Christian doth as it were begin the day of judgment here in his own soul. Self-searching is a heart-anatomy. As a surgeon, when he makes a dissection in the body, discovers the *intestina* – the inward parts – the heart, liver, arteries, so a Christian anatomizeth himself. He searcheth what is flesh, and what is spirit, what is sin, and what is grace. 'My spirit made diligent search' (Psa. 77:6). As the woman in the gospel did light a candle and search for her lost coin (Luke

---

[1] [That is, lack.]

15:8), so conscience 'is the candle of the Lord' (Prov. 20:27). A Christian by the light of this candle must search his soul, if he can find any grace there. The rule by which a Christian must try himself is the word of God. Fancy and opinion are false rules to go by. We must judge of our spiritual condition by the canon of Scripture. This David calls a 'lamp unto his feet' (Psa. 119:105). Let the word be the umpire to decide the controversy whether we have grace or not. We judge of colours by the sun, so we must judge of the estate of souls by the light of Scripture.

Self-examination is a great duty incumbent; it requires self-excitation: it cannot possibly be done without offering violence to ourselves.

(i) *Because the duty in itself is difficult:* [1] It is *actus reflexivus,* a work of *self-reflection*. It lies most with the heart. It is hard to look inward. External acts of religion are facile – to lift up the eye to heaven, to bow the knee, to read a prayer; this requires no more labour than for a Catholic to tell over his beads; but to examine a man's self, to turn in upon his own soul, to take the heart as a watch all in pieces, and see what is defective; this is not easy. Reflective acts are hardest. The eye can see everything but itself. It is easy to spy the faults of others, but hard to find out our own. [2] Examination of a man's self is difficult, *because of self-love*. As ignorance blinds, so self-love flatters. Every man is ready to think the best of himself. What Solomon saith of love to our neighbour, is most true of self-love; it 'hides a multitude of evil' (Prov. 10:12). A man looking upon himself in *Philautae speculo,* in the glass of self-love, his virtues appear greater than they are, and his sins lesser. Self-love makes one rather excuse what is amiss, than examine it.

(ii) *As examination is in itself difficult, so it is a work which we are very hardly brought to.* That which causeth a backwardness to self-examination, is,

[1] *Consciousness of guilt.* Sin clamours inwardly, and men are loath to look into their hearts, lest they should find that which should trouble them. It is little pleasure to read the handwriting on the wall of conscience. Many Christians are like tradesmen that are sinking in their estates; they are loath to look over their books, or cast up their accounts, lest they should find their estates low: so they are loath to look into their guilty heart, lest they should find something there which should frighten them: as Moses was frightened at the sight of the rod turned into a serpent.

[2] Men are hardly brought to this duty because of *foolish presumptuous hopes:* they fancy their estate to be good, and while they weigh themselves in the balance of presumption, they pass for current. Many take their salvation on trust. The foolish virgins thought they had oil in their lamps, as well as the wise (Matt. 25). Some are not sure of their salvation, but secure. If one were to buy a piece of land, he would not take it upon trust, but examine the title. How confident are some of salvation, yet never examine their title to heaven.

[3] Men are not forward to examine themselves because *they rest in the good opinion of others.* How vain is this! Alas, one may be gold and pearl in the eye of others, yet God may judge him reprobate silver: others may think him a saint, and God may write him down in his black book. Judas was looked upon by the rest of the apostles as a true believer; they would have been ready to have given their hands to this certificate; yet he was a traitor. Bystanders can but see

the outward carriage; they cannot tell what evil is in the heart. Fair streams may run on the top of a river, but vermin may lay at the bottom.

[4] Men are hardly brought to examine themselves because *they do not believe Scripture*. The Scripture saith, 'The heart is deceitful above all things' (Jer. 17:9). Solomon said there were four things too wonderful for him that he could not know (Prov. 30:19). He might have added a fifth, the way of man's heart. The heart is the greatest impostor; it will be ready to put one off with seeming grace, instead of saving. The heart will persuade that a slight tear is repentance, a lazy desire is faith. Now because the generality of people do not believe that there is such fallacy in their hearts, therefore they are so slow to examine them. This natural backwardness in us to self-reflection should cause us to offer the more violence to ourselves in making a thorough disquisition and search of our hearts.

Oh that I might prevail with Christians to take pains with themselves in this great work of examination! Their salvation depends on it. It is the note of a harlot; she is seldom at home: 'Her feet abide not in her house; now is she without, now in the streets' (Prov. 7:11, 12). It is a sign of a harlot-professor to be altogether abroad, spying the faults of others; but is never at home with his own heart. Oh let us try our hearts, as we do gold by the touchstone! Let us examine our sins, and finding out this leaven, burn it. Let us examine our grace, whether it be of the right kind. One went into the field to gather herbs, and he gathered 'wild gourds,' and then 'death was in the pot' (2 Kings 4:39, 40). So many think they have grace, the right herb; but it proves a wild gourd, and brings death and damnation.

OR, THE CHRISTIAN SOLDIER

That we may offer violence to ourselves in this great business of examination, let these few things be seriously weighed:

First, Without self-examination *we can never know how it is with us*. If we should die presently, we cannot tell to what coast we should sail, whether to hell or heaven. It is reported of Socrates, when he was going out of the world, he had this speech: 'I am now to die, and the gods know whether I shall be happy or miserable.' That man who is ignorant of the state of his soul, must needs have the trembling at the heart (1 Sam. 4:13; Job 37:1), as Cain had a shaking in his flesh. By a serious scrutiny of our hearts, we come to know to what prince we belong, whether the prince of peace (Isa. 9:6), or the prince of the air (Eph. 2:2).

Second, If we will not try ourselves, *God will try us*. He will examine us as the chief captain did Paul, 'by scourging' (Acts 22:24). He will ask that question as Christ, 'Whose image and superscription is this?' (Matt. 22:20). And if we cannot show him his own image, he will reject us.

Third, *There is secret corruption within, which will never be found out but by searching*. There is in the heart (as Augustine saith) hidden pollution. When Pharaoh's steward accused Joseph's brethren of having the cup, they durst have sworn they had not the cup in their sacks. Little doth a man know what atheism, pride, uncleanness is in his heart, till he searcheth.

Fourth, *The great advantage which will accrue to us:* the benefit is great which way soever things turn. If upon examination we find that we have not grace in truth, then the mistake is discovered, and the danger prevented. If we find that we have grace, we may take the comfort of it. How glad was he that had found 'the pearl of great price'? He that upon search finds that he hath but the *minimum quod sic,* the least degree of grace, is like one that hath found his box of evidences; he is heir to all the promises, and in a state of salvation.

And that we may go on the more successfully in this work, let us desire God to help us to find out our hearts, 'that which I see not teach thou me' (Job 34:32). Lord, take off the veil; show me my heart; let me not perish through mistake, or go to hell with hope of heaven.

The 6th duty wherein we must offer violence to ourselves, is, the religious sanctifying of the Lord's day.

That there should be a day of holy rest dedicated to God, appears from the institution, 'Remember to keep holy the sabbath day.' Our Christian sabbath comes in the room of the Jewish sabbath. It is called, 'the Lord's day' (Rev. 1:10), from Christ the author of it. Our sabbath is altered by Christ's own appointment. He arose this day out of the grave, and appeared on it often to his disciples (John 20:19). To intimate to them (saith Athanasius) that he transferred the sabbath to the Lord's day. And St Augustine saith, that by Christ's rising on the first day of the week, it was consecrated to be the Christian sabbath, in remembrance of his resurrection. This day was anciently called *dies lucis,* the day of light, as Junius observes. The other days of the week would be dark, were it not for the shining of the Sun of Righteousness on this day. This day hath been called by the ancients, *regina dierum,* the queen of days. And St Jerome prefers this day above all solemn festivals. The primitive church had this day in high veneration. It was a great badge of their religion, for when the question was asked, *Servasti dominicum?* Keepest thou the sabbath? the answer was made, *Christianus sum,* I am a Christian, and dare not omit the celebration of the Lord's day. What great cause have we thankfully to remember this day! As the benefit of Israel's deliverance from the Babylonish captivity was so great, that it drowned the remembrance of their deliverance from Egypt (Jer. 16:14); so the benefit of our deliverance from Satan's captivity, and the rising of Christ from finishing the glorious work of our redemption, was so famous, that in respect of his other benefits, receive as it were a diminution. Great was the work of creation, but greater the work of redemption. It cost more to redeem us than make us. In the one there was only the speaking a word (Psa. 148:5), in the other the shedding of blood (Heb. 9:22). The creation was the work of God's fingers (Psa. 8:3), the redemption, the work of his arm (Luke 1:51). In the creation God gave us ourselves, in the redemption he gave us himself. So that the sabbath, putting us in mind of our redemption, ought to be so served with the highest devotion. Herein we must offer holy violence to ourselves.

When this blessed day approacheth, we should labour, that as the day is sanctified, so our hearts may be sanctified.

We must on this day rest from all the works of our calling; as Abraham when he went to sacrifice, left his servant and ass at the bottom of the hill (Gen. 22:5). So when we are to worship God this day, we must leave all secular business behind. And as Joseph when he would speak with his brethren, thrust out the Egyptians, so when we would have converse with God this day, we must thrust out all earthly employments. Though works of necessity may be done, and works of charity (for God will have mercy and not sacrifice), yet in other cases we must cease from all worldly negotiations. It is observable concerning Mary Magdalene, that she refused to anoint Christ's dead body on the sabbath day (Luke 23:56). She had before prepared her ointment, but came not to the sepulchre till the sabbath was past. She rested that day from civil work, though it were a commendable and glorious work; the anointing of Christ's dead body.

When this blessed day approacheth, we must lift up our heart in thankfulness to God, that he hath put another price into our hands for the gaining of heavenly wisdom. These are our spiritual harvest-days; now the wind of God's Spirit blows upon the sails of our affections, and we may be much furthered on in our heavenly voyage. Christian, lift up thy heart to God in thankfulness, that he hath given thee another golden season, and be sure thou improve it; it may be the last. Seasons of grace are not like the tide; if a man misseth one tide, he may have another.

This day approaching, we must, in the morning, dress and fit our souls for the receiving of the word. The people of Israel must wash their garments before the law was delivered to them. Our hearts must be washed by prayer and repentance, the oracles of God being delivered to us.

And being met together, we must set ourselves as in the presence of God with seriousness and delight to hear God's sacred word. Take heed of distractions which fly-blow our duties.

We must labour to be bettered by every sabbath: where the Lord lays out cost, he looks for fruit. Fresh anointings of God are to be thirsted after, and new cubits to be added to our spiritual stature. We must not be like the salamander, which lives in the fire but is never the hotter. Christians should on these days aspire after communion with God, and endeavour to have the illapses[1] of his Spirit and clearer discoveries of his love in Christ. In short, we should do on a sabbath as Moses; he ascended the mount that he might have a sight of God.

We must dedicate the whole day to God. Under the law a single sacrifice was appointed for other days of the week; but two lambs were to be offered upon the sabbath. All this day must be spent with God. He must have worship in the public, and when we come home he must have family worship. Many leave all their religion at church (as I have seen some do their Bibles), not hallowing God's name in their own houses. 'Will a man rob God?' (Mal. 3:8). When men pretend to worship God in the temple, but cut him short of family and closet duties on a sabbath, this is to rob God and steal part of his day from him.

Good reason we should consecrate the whole sabbath to God and give him double devotion, for God doubles his blessings upon us this day. As the manna did rain twice as much on the sixth day, as any of the other days, so the manna of spiritual blessings falls twice as much on the sabbath day as any other.

We must rejoice in this day, as being a day wherein we enjoy much of God's presence. 'Abraham saw my day and rejoiced' (John 8:56). So when we see a sabbath day coming, we should rejoice. The Protestants in France called their church 'Paradise,' because there they met with God. The Jews called the sabbath, *desiderium dierum,* the desire of days: 'Thou shalt call the sabbath a delight' (Isa. 58:13). This we should look upon as the best day, as the queen of days

---

[1] [Illapses: influx or inflow.]

crowned with a blessing. 'This is the day which the Lord hath made; we will rejoice and be glad in it' (Psa. 118:24). He hath made all the days, but hath sanctified this. We should look upon this day as a spiritual mart for our souls, wherein we have holy commerce and traffic with God. This day of rest is the beginning of an eternal rest. This day God sets open the pool of Bethesda, in which those waters flow that refresh the broken in heart. And shall not we call this a delight? The Jews on the sabbath laid aside their sackcloth and mourning.

This is in a right manner to sanctify a duty; and it is a duty wherein Christians must excite and offer violence to themselves.

Above all others, how well doth it become those into whose hands God hath put the power of magistracy to show forth holy violence in causing the Lord's day to be strictly observed? What a rare pattern hath Nehemiah set all good magistrates: 'In those days saw I in Judah some treading winepresses on the sabbath, and bringing in sheaves, and all manner of burdens which they brought into Jerusalem on the sabbath day, and I testified against them in the day wherein they sold victuals' (Neh. 13:15). 'Then I contended with the nobles of Judea, and said unto them, What evil thing is this that ye do, and profane the sabbath day?' (Neh. 13:17). How dare ye infringe the command, and make a false entry upon God's freehold? My lord, your proclamation for the pious observation of the sabbath and your punitive acts upon some offenders, have given a public testimony of your zeal for this day. The keeping up the honour of the sabbath will much keep up your magisterial honour.

The 7th duty wherein we must offer violence to ourselves, is holy conference; and indeed we are backward enough to

OR, THE CHRISTIAN SOLDIER

it, therefore had need herein provoke ourselves, 'They that feared the Lord spake often one to another' (Mal. 3:16).

A gracious person hath not only religion in his heart, but in his tongue, 'The law of God is in his heart, and his tongue talketh of judgment' (Psa. 37:30, 31). He drops holy words as pearls. It is the fault of Christians that they do not in company provoke themselves to set good discourse on foot. It is a sinful modesty. There is much visiting, but they do not give one another's souls a visit. In worldly things their tongue is as the pen of a ready writer; but in matters of religion, they are as if their tongue did cleave to the roof of their mouth. As we must answer to God for idle words, so for sinful silence.

Oh let us offer violence to ourselves on this, in setting abroach good discourse! What should our words dilate and expatiate upon but heaven? The world is a great inn; we are guests in this inn. Travellers, when they are met in their inn, do not spend all their time in speaking about their inn; they are to lodge there but a few hours, and they are gone; but they are speaking of their home, and the country whither they are travelling. So when we meet together, we should not be talking only about the world; we are to leave this presently; but we should talk of our heavenly country (Heb. 11:16).

That we may provoke ourselves to good discourse (for it will not be done without some kind of violence) let these considerations be duly weighed.

The discourse demonstrates what the heart is. As the glass shows what the face is, whether it be fair or foul, so the words show what the heart is. Vain speeches discover a light feathery heart; gracious speeches are the birth of a gracious heart. The water of the conduit shows what the spring is.

Holy conference is very edifying. The apostle bids us 'edify one another' (Eph. 4:29). And how more than this way? Good conference enlightens the mind when it is ignorant; settles it when it is wavering. A good life adorns religion; good discourse propagates it.

Gracious discourse makes us resemble Christ. His words were perfumed with holiness: 'grace was poured into his lips' (Psa. 45:2). He spake to the admiration of all. His hands wrought miracles and his tongue spake oracles. 'All bare him witness, and wondered at the gracious words which proceeded out of his mouth' (Luke 4:22). Christ never came into any company, but he set good discourse on foot. Levi made him a feast (Luke 5:29), and Christ feasted him with holy discourse. When he came to Jacob's well, he presently speaks of the 'water of life' (John 4:10-14). The more holy our speeches are, the more we are like Christ. Should not the members be like the head?

God takes special notice of every good word we speak when we meet: 'They that feared the Lord spake often one to another; and the Lord hearkened and heard, and a book of remembrance was written before him' (Mal. 3:16). Tamerlain, that Scythian captain, had always a book by him of the names and good works of his servants which he bountifully rewarded. As God hath a bottle for the tears of his people, so he hath a book in which he writes down all their good speeches, and will make honourable mention of them at the last day.

Holy discourse will be a means to bring Christ into our company. The two disciples were communing of the death and sufferings of Christ; and while they were speaking, Jesus Christ came among them: 'While they communed together, Jesus himself drew near, and went with them' (Luke 24:15). When men entertain bad discourse Satan draws near, and he makes one of the company; but when they have holy and gracious conference, Jesus Christ draws near, and wherever he comes, he brings a blessing along with him. So much for the first, the offering violence to ourselves.

II. We Must Offer Violence to Satan

SATAN opposeth us both by open *violence*, and secret *treachery*. By open violence, so he is called the red dragon; by secret treachery, so he is called the old serpent. We read in Scripture of his 'snares' and 'darts'; he hurts more by his snares than by his darts.

1. Satan's violence

He labours to storm the castle of the heart: he stirs up to passion, lust, revenge. These are called 'fiery darts' (Eph. 6:16), because they oft set the soul on fire. Satan in regard to his fierceness is called a lion: 'Your adversary the devil, as a roaring lion, walketh about, seeking whom he may devour' (1 Pet. 5:8). Not (saith Chrysostom) whom he may *bite* but *devour*.

2. Satan's treachery

What he cannot do by *force*, he will endeavour to do by *fraud*. Satan hath several subtle policies in tempting.

(1) *In suiting his temptations to the complexion and temper of the body.* Satan studies the physiognomy, and lays suitable baits. He knew Achan's covetous humour, and

tempted him with a wedge of gold. He tempts the sanguine man with beauty.

(2) *Another subtlety is to draw men to evil,* sub specie boni, *under a pretence of good.* The pirate doth mischief by hanging out false colours; so doth Satan by hanging out the colours of religion. He puts some men upon sinful actions and persuades them much good will come of it. He tells them in some cases they may dispense with the rule of the word, and stretch their conscience beyond that line, that they may be in a capacity of doing more service. As if God needed our sin to raise his glory.

(3) *Satan tempts to sin gradually.* As the husbandman digs about the root of a tree, and by degrees loosens it, and at last it falls, Satan steals by degrees into the heart. He is at first more modest. He did not say to Eve at first, 'Eat the apple'; no, but he goes more subtly to work. He puts forth a question, 'Hath God said?' Sure Eve, thou art mistaken; the bountiful God never intended to debar thee one of the best trees of the garden. 'Hath God said?' Sure, either God did not say it; or if he did, he never really intended it. Thus by degrees he wrought her to distrust, and then she took of the fruit and did eat. Oh, take heed of Satan's first motions to sin that seem more modest – *principiis obsta*.[1] He is first a fox, and then a lion.

(4) *Satan tempts to evil* in licitis, *in lawful things.* It was lawful for Noah to eat the fruit of the grape; but he took too much, and so sinned. Excess turns that which is good into evil. Eating and drinking may turn to intemperance. Industry in one's calling (when excessive) is covetousness. Satan draws men to an immoderate love of the creature, and then

[1] [Resist the beginnings (of temptation).]

makes them offend in that which they love. As Agrippina poisoned her husband Claudius in that food he loved most.

(5) *Satan puts men upon doing good out of bad ends:* if he cannot hurt them by scandalous actions, he will by virtuous actions. Thus he tempts some to espouse religion out of policy to get preferment, and to give alms, for applause, that others may see their good works, and canonize them. This hypocrisy doth leaven the duties of religion, and make them lose their reward.

(6) *The devil persuades to evil by such as are good.* This sets a gloss upon his temptations, and makes them less suspected. The devil hath made use sometimes of the eminentest and holiest men to promote his temptations. The devil tempted Christ by an apostle; Peter dissuades him from suffering. Abraham, a good man, bids his wife equivocate: 'Say, Thou art my sister.' These are his subtleties in tempting.

Now here we must offer violence to Satan,

1. *By faith:* 'Whom resist, steadfast in faith' (1 Pet. 5:9). Faith is a wise, intelligent grace; it can see a hook under the bait. It is an heroic grace; it is said, above all, to quench the fiery darts of Satan.

Faith resists the devil. (1) As it doth keep the castle of the heart *that it doth not yield*. It is not the being tempted makes guilty; but giving consent. Faith enters its protest against Satan. (2) Faith not only not yields, but *beats back the temptation*. Faith holds the promise in one hand, and Christ in the other: the promise encourageth faith, and Christ strengthens it: so faith beats the enemy out of the field.

2. *By prayer.* We must offer violence to Satan by prayer. We overcome him upon our knees. As Samson called to

heaven for help, so a Christian, by prayer fetcheth in auxiliary forces from heaven. In all temptations go to God by prayer. 'Lord, teach me to use every piece of the spiritual armour; how to hold the shield, how to wear the helmet, how to use the sword of the Spirit. Lord, strengthen me in the battle; let me rather die a conqueror, than be taken prisoner, and led by Satan in triumph.' Thus we must offer violence to Satan. There is 'a lion in the way' (Prov. 22:13), but we must resolve upon fighting.

And let this encourage us to offer violence to Satan. Our enemy is beaten in part already. Christ, who is 'the captain of our salvation,' hath given Satan his death-wound upon the cross (Col. 2:15). The serpent is soonest killed in his head. Christ hath bruised the head of the old Serpent. The devil is a chained enemy, and a conquered enemy; therefore fear not to give battle to him. Resist him, and he will fly (James 4:7): he knows no march but running away.

III. We Must Offer Violence to the World

THE world shows its golden apple, it is a part of our vow in baptism to fight under Christ's banner against the world. Take heed of being drowned in the luscious delights of it. It must be a strong brain that bears heady wine. He had need have a great deal of wisdom and grace, that knows how to bear a great estate. Riches oft send up their intoxicating fumes, which makes men's heads giddy with pride: 'Jeshurun waxed fat and kicked' (Deut. 32:15). It is hard to climb up the hill of God with too many golden weights. Those that want[1] the honours of the world, want the temptations of it. The world is *blandus Daemon,* a flattering enemy. It is given

[1] [That is, lack.]

to some, as Michal to David, for a snare. The world shows its two breasts of pleasure and profit, and many fall asleep with the breast in their mouth. The world doth never kiss us, but with an intent to betray us. It is a silken halter. The world is no friend to grace; it chokes our love to heavenly things; the earth puts out the fire. Naturally we love the world: 'If I have made gold my hope' (Job 31:24); the Septuagint renders it, 'If I have been married to my gold.' Too many are wedded to their money; they live together, as man and wife. Oh let us take heed of being entangled in this pleasing snare! Many who have escaped the rock of scandalous sins, yet have sunk in the world's golden quicksands. The sin is not in the *using* of the world, but in the *loving*. 'Love not the world' (1 John 2:15). If we are Christians, we must offer violence to the world. Believers are 'called out of the world.' They are *in* the world, but not *of* it (John 17:16). As we say of a dying man, he is not a man for this world. A true saint is crucified in his affections to the world (Gal. 6:14); he is dead to the honours and treasures of it. What delight doth a dead man take in pictures or music? Jesus Christ gave himself 'to redeem us from this present evil world' (Gal. 1:4). If we will be saved, we must offer violence to the world. Living fish swim against the stream. We must swim against the world, else we shall be carried down the stream, and fall into the dead sea.

That we may offer violence to the world, let us remember:

1. The world is *deceitful*. Our 'Saviour calls it, 'the deceitfulness of riches' (Matt. 13:22). The world promiseth happiness, but nothing less. It promiseth us Rachel, but puts us off with blear-eyed Leah; it promiseth to satisfy our desires, but it increaseth them; it gives poisoned pills, but wraps them in sugar.

2. The world is *defiling*. 'Pure religion is to keep himself unspotted from the world' (James 1:27). As if the apostle would intimate, that the world is good for nothing but to spot. It first spots men's consciences, and then their names. It is called 'filthy lucre' (1 Pet. 5:2), because it makes men so filthy. They will damn themselves to get the world. Ahab would have Naboth's vineyard, though he swam to it in blood.

3. The world is *perishing*. 'The fashion of the world passeth away' (1 Cor. 7:31; 1 John 2:17). The world is like a flower which withers while we are smelling it.

IV. We Must Offer Violence to Heaven

WE must offer violence to heaven. 'The kingdom of heaven suffereth violence.' Though heaven is given us freely, yet we must take pains for it. Canaan was given to Israel freely, but they must fight with the Canaanites. It is not a lazy wish, or sleepy prayer that will bring us to heaven; we must offer violence. Therefore in Scripture our earnestness for heaven is set out by those allegories and metaphors which imply violence:

1. Sometimes *by striving*: 'Strive to enter in at the straight gate' (Luke 13:24). The Greek signifies strive as in an agony.

2. *Wrestling*, which is a violent exercise. We are to wrestle with a body of sin and with the powers of hell (Eph. 6:12).

3. *Running in a race*. 'So run, that ye may obtain' (1 Cor. 9:24). We have a long race from earth to heaven, and but a little time to run; it will soon be sunset. Therefore so run. In a race there's not only laying aside all weights that hinder, but a putting forth all the strength of the body; a straining of every joint that men may press on with all swiftness to lay

hold on the prize. Thus St Paul 'pressed towards the mark' (Phil. 3:14).

Alas! where is this holy violence to be found?

1. *Many have made themselves unfit to run this blessed race*. They are drunk with the pleasures of the world. A drunken man is unfit to run a race.

2. *Others neglect to run this race all their life; and when sickness and death approach, now they will begin*. A sick man is very unfit to walk, much less, to run a race. I acknowledge true repentance is never too late; but when a man can hardly stir his hand, or lift up his eyes, now is a very unfit time to begin the race from earth to heaven.

3. *This earnestness for heaven is compared to fighting, which implies violence*: 'Fight the good fight of faith' (1 Tim. 6:12). It is not enough to be labourers, but warriors. Indeed in heaven, our armour shall be hung up in token of victory; but now it is *dies praelii*, a day of battle; and we must 'fight the good fight of faith.' As Hannibal forced a way for his army over the Alps and craggy rocks, so must we force our way to heaven. We must not only pray, but pray fervently (James 5:16). This is offering violence to heaven.

The *reasons* why there must be this offering violence to heaven, are:

1. *God's indispensable command*. He hath enacted a law, that whosoever eats of the fruit of paradise, shall eat it in the sweat of his brow: 'Give diligence to make your calling and election sure' (2 Pet. 1:10).

2. *God's decree*. The Lord hath in his eternal decree joined the end and the means together: striving and entering, the race and the crown. And a man can no more think

[53]

to come to heaven without offering violence, than he can think to come to the end of his journey that never sets a step in the way. Who expects a harvest without ploughing and sowing? How can we expect the harvest of glory without labour? Though our salvation in respect of Christ is a purchase, yet in respect of us it is a conquest.

3. We must offer violence to heaven in regard of *the difficulty of the work: taking a kingdom*. First, *we must be pulled out of another kingdom,* 'the kingdom of darkness' (Acts 26:18). To get out of the state of nature is hard, and when that is done, and we are cut off from the wild olive, and implanted into Christ, there is *new work still to do*: new sins to mortify, new temptations to resist, new graces to quicken. A Christian must not only get faith, but go 'from faith to faith' (Rom. 1:17). This will not be done without violence.

4. We must offer violence to heaven, in regard of *the violent assaults made against us*. (1) *Our own hearts* oppose us. It is a strange paradox: man, who doth naturally desire happiness, yet opposeth it: he desires to be saved, yet hates that holy violence which should save him. (2) *All the powers of hell* oppose us. Satan stands at our right hand, as he did at Joshua's (Zech. 3:1). Shall we not be as earnest to save our souls, as the dragon is to devour them? Without violent affections we shall never resist violent temptations.

5. We must be violent, because it is a *matter of the highest importance*. A man doth not beat his head about trifles, but matters wherein his life and estate is concerned. Violence is to be offered, if we consider:

(1) *What we shall save: a precious soul*. What pains do we take for the feeding and enriching the body, the

brutish part? Oh then what violence should we use for the saving the soul? The body is but a ring of clay, the soul is the diamond. The soul is the glass wherein the image of God is seen. There are in the soul some shadows and faint representations of a deity. If Christ thought the soul worth shedding his blood, well may we think it worth spending our sweat.

(2) *Consider what we shall gain: a kingdom.* What violence is used for earthly crowns and empires! Men will wade to the crown through blood. Heaven is a kingdom which should make us strive for it, *Non ad sudorem tantum sed sanguinem*,[1] even to blood. The hopes of a kingdom, saith St Basil, should carry a Christian cheerfully through all labours and sufferings.

There must be offering violence in regard of that aptness and proneness in the best to grow remiss in religion. When they have been quickened in a duty, they are apt to grow dead again. When they have been heated at the fire of an ordinance, they are apt to freeze again; therefore they must be still offering violence. The heart, like the watch, will be apt to go down. Therefore it must be ever and anon wound up by prayer and meditation. The fire of devotion will soon go out, if it be not blown up.

A Christian's own experience of his inconstancy in good, is cogent enough to holy violence.

If there must be this offering violence, it shows us it is not so easy a thing as men imagine to get to heaven. There are so many precepts to obey, so many promises to believe, so many rocks to avoid, that it is a difficult matter to be saved. Some fancy a fine easy way to heaven, an idle wish,

[1] [Not only to sweat, but to blood.]

a death-bed tear. But the text tells us of offering violence. Alas, there is a great work to be done! The bias of the heart is to be changed. Man by nature not only wants grace, but hates it. He hath an envenomed spirit against goodness, and is angry with converting grace. And is it easy to have the heart metamorphosed? For the proud heart to be made humble? For the earthly heart to be made heavenly? Can this be done without using violence? It is all uphill to heaven, and it will make us sweat before we get to the top of the hill. Indeed hell will be taken without storm. The gates of hell, like that iron gate, open of their own accord (Acts 12:10). But if we get to heaven we must force our way. We must besiege it with sighs and tears, and get the scaling ladder of faith to storm it. We must not only work, but fight. Like those Jews, who built the wall of Jerusalem: 'Every one with one of his hands wrought in the work, and with the other hand held a weapon' (Neh. 4:17). A Christian is commanded upon hot service. He must charge through the whole army of his lusts, every one of which is stronger than Goliath. A Christian hath no time to lie fallow. He must be either praying or watching – either upon the mount, or in the valley – on the mount of faith, or in the valley of humility. Worldly things are not obtained without labour – what toiling in the shop, what sweating in the furnace! – and do we think heaven will be had without labour? Do men dig for worms, and not for gold? Those who are in heaven are employed; much more should they who are getting thither. The angels are 'ministering spirits' (Heb. 1:14). The wings of the seraphims are hierogliphical, and show us how swift they are in God's service. If the angels in heaven are busying themselves in noble and honourable employment, how

OR, THE CHRISTIAN SOLDIER

industrious should we be who are getting up the hill of God, and have not yet arrived at a state of glory? Is salvation-work so easy? Can a man be saved by a leap? Can he leap out of the devil's arms into Abraham's bosom? Oh no, there must be offering violence. Some think free grace will save them; but it must be in the use of means. 'Watch and pray' (Matt. 26:41). Others say, the promises will bring them to heaven. But the promises of the word are not to be separated from the precepts. The promise tells us of a crown, but the precept saith, 'So run' (1 Cor. 9:24). The promises are made to encourage faith, not to cherish sloth. But, say others, Christ hath died for sinners; and so they leave him to do all for them, and they will do nothing. Then the text is out of date! and all the exhortations to striving, and 'fighting the good fight of faith' are in vain! Our salvation cost Christ's blood; it will cost us sweat. The boat may as well get to shore without rowing, as we can to heaven without offering violence.

It shows us the great mistake of ignorant people, who think the bare doing of duties, though in never so slight, superficial a manner, is enough. The text tells us of offering violence:

(1) In *the business of prayer*. They think it is enough to utter over a few words, though the heart be asleep all the while. What offering of violence is here? Christ was 'in an agony' at prayer (Luke 22:44): many when they pray are rather in a lethargy than in an agony! Jacob wrestled with the angel in prayer (Gen. 32:24). The incense was to be laid upon burning coals (Lev. 16:12, 13). Incense was a type of prayer, and the incense upon coals was a type of fervency in prayer. Few know what the spirit of prayer means, or what

it is to have the affections boil over. When they are about the world they are all fire; when they are at prayer they are all ice.

(2) In *hearing of the word*. Many people think it is enough to bring their bodies to the assembly, but they never look to their hearts. They satisfy themselves that they have been at church, though they have not been with God there. Others go to a sermon as to the exchange, to hear news; new notions that please their fancy, but do not attend to the word as about a matter of life and death. They do not go to meet with Christ in an ordinance, to have the breathings of his Spirit, and the infusions of his love. Alas, what little violence for heaven is to be seen in most people's worship! In all the sacrifices of the law there was fire. How can those duties be accepted, which have no fuel in them, no offering of violence?

If there must be this offering of violence to heaven, then it shows us how dangerous moderation in religion is. Violence and moderation are two different things. Indeed moderation in the things of the world is commendable. We should moderate our desires here, and 'use the world as if we used it not' (1 Cor. 7:31). We may, as Jonathan, dip the end of the rod in honey, but not thrust it in too far. In this sense moderation is good. But moderation in matters of practical piety is sinful. It is contrary to offering violence. Moderation, in the world's sense, is for one not to be too zealous, not to be too fierce for heaven. Moderation is not to venture further in religion than may stand with self-preservation. As the king of Navarre told Beza, he would launch no further into the sea, than he might be sure to return safe to land. To keep on the warm side of the hedge is a main article in the politician's creed. Moderation in the world's sense is neutrality. The moderate person hath found out a medium between strictness and profaneness: he is not for debauchery, nor yet for purity. It was the advice Calvin gave Melanchthon, that he should not so affect the name of moderate, that at last he lost all his zeal. To be lukewarm in matters of religion, is far from offering violence to heaven: 'Be zealous and repent' (Rev. 3:19). If any should ask us why we are so violent, tell them, It is for a kingdom. If any shall ask us why we make such haste in the ways of religion, tell them, We are running a heavenly race, and a softly moderate pace will never win the prize. Moderation hath made many lose heaven; they have not made haste enough; they have come too late (like the foolish virgins) when the door hath been shut.

Reproofs Arising from the Text

Out of this text I may draw forth several arrows of reproof.

1. It reproves *slothful Christians* who are settled on their lees (Zeph. 1:12). They make a lazy profession of religion, but use no violence. They are like the lilies, which toil not, neither do they spin. The snail by reason of its slow motion, was reckoned among the unclean (Lev. 11:30). St Augustine calls idleness the burial of a man alive. There are some faint wishes: 'Oh that I had heaven!' – but a man may desire venison, and want it,[1] if he doth not hunt for it: 'The soul of the sluggard wisheth and hath nothing' (Prov. 13:4).

Neque mola, neque farina.[2]

[1] [That is, lack it.]
[2] [Without the millstone, there is no flour.]

Men could be content to have the kingdom of heaven, but they are loath to fight for it. They choose rather to go in a feather bed to hell, than to be carried to heaven in a fiery chariot of zeal and violence. How many sleep away, and play away their time; as if they were made like the leviathan, to play in the sea (Psa. 104:26)! It is a speech of Seneca, 'No man is made wise by chance.' Sure it is no man is saved by chance, but he must know how he came by it, namely, by offering violence. Such as have accustomed themselves to an idle lazy temper will find it hard to shake it off: 'I have put off my coat, how shall I put it on?' (Song of Sol. 5:3). The spouse had laid herself upon the bed of sloth, and though Christ knocked at the door, she was loath to rise and let him in. Some pretend to be believers, but are idle in the vineyard. They pretend to make use of faith for seeing, but not for working; this faith is fancy. Oh that Christians had a spirit of activity in them! 'Arise and be doing, and the Lord be with thee' (1 Chron. 22:16).

We may sometimes learn of our enemy. The devil is never idle: he 'walketh about' (1 Pet. 5:8). The world is his diocese, and he is every day going his visitation. Is Satan active, is the enemy upon his march coming against us, and are we asleep upon our guard? As Satan himself is not idle, so he will not endure that any of his servants should be idle. When the devil had entered into Judas, how active was Judas! He goes to the high priest, from thence to the band of soldiers, and with them back to the garden, and never left till he had betrayed Christ. Satan will not endure an idle servant, and do we think God will? How will heathens rise up in judgment against slothful Christians! What pains did they take in the Olympian games! They ran for a garland

OR, THE CHRISTIAN SOLDIER

of flowers. And do we stand still who run for a crown of immortality? Certainly, if only the violent take heaven, the idle person will never come there. God puts no difference between these two, slothful and wicked: 'Thou wicked and slothful servant' (Matt. 25:26).

2. It reproves the *formalist,* who puts all his religion in gestures and vestures, emblems of devotion, and thinks this will entitle him to heaven, 'Thou hast a name to live and art dead' (Rev. 3:1). The form and outside of Christianity is judged necessary.

(1) *It is a means to keep men's credit in the world.* Should they be visibly profane, such as are sober would not come near them. They would be looked upon no better than baptized heathens. Therefore they must make a show of devotion, out of policy to gain some repute and esteem among others.

(2) *A form serves to stop the mouth of conscience.* Had not they some kind of outward devotion, their conscience would fly in their face, and they would be a terror to themselves. Therefore they think it expedient to have a form of godliness. But alas, what is all this? The text speaks of offering violence to heaven. What violence is there in a form? Here is no taking pains with the heart: a 'form,' but no 'power' (2 Tim. 3:5). Formalists are like the tombs in the church, which have their eyes and hands lifted up to heaven, but no soul. The formalist's devotion runs out most in punctilios and niceties: he neglects 'the weightier matter of the law, faith and mercy' (Matt. 23:23). He scruples superstitious fancies, but makes no reckoning of sin. He is more afraid of a hare crossing his way than of a harlot in his

bed. He hates sanctity. Christ had no such bitter enemies as the formal Pharisees. The formalist is never violent, but in persecuting the power of godliness.

3. It reproves such as are violent in a *bad sense:* they are violent for hell; they go thither in the sweat of their brows: 'Every one turned to his course, as the horse rusheth into the battle' (Jer. 8:6). A war-horse rusheth violently among the guns and pikes: so did they rush into sin violently.

Men are violent, (1) In opposing good and (2) In pursuing evil.

(1) *In opposing good.* Several ways.

(i) They offer violence to *the Spirit of God.* The Spirit knocks at the door of sinners' hearts; he waits till his head be 'filled with dew,' and 'his locks with the drops of the night'; but sinners repulse and grieve the Spirit, and send away this dove from the ark of their souls: 'Ye do always resist the Holy Ghost' (Acts 7:51). The Spirit offers grace to the sinner, and the sinner offers violence to the Spirit: 'They rebelled and vexed his holy Spirit' (Isa. 63:10); and may not the Lord give over striving? God, who is willing to come in when we open to him, hath not promised to come again if we unkindly repulse him.

(ii) They offer violence to *conscience.* Conscience is God's preacher in the bosom; and this preacher cannot flatter: it tells men of their pride, covetousness, abuse of mercy. But they, instead of being violent against their sins, offer violence to conscience. They silence and imprison conscience. But as the prophet Zacharias, when he was dumb called for a writing table, and did write (Luke 1:63), so when conscience cannot be permitted to speak, it will write.

It writes down men's sins. And when at death they shall be forced to read the handwriting, it will make their hearts tremble and their knees smite. This I fear is too common, for men to offer violence to their conscience. And what will be the issue? They who will not hear the voice of conscience shall be sure to feel the worm of conscience.

(iii) They offer violence to *God's image*. The saints (who are God's lively picture) are opposed and shot at. This is a cursed violence: 'As he that was born after the flesh, persecuted him who was born after the Spirit; so it is now' (Gal. 4:29). Christ himself is stricken at through believers. The church hath been always in the torrid zone: the ploughers have ploughed upon her back. The earth hath been sown with the bodies of the saints and watered with their blood. Persecutors, I grant, are of an ancient family. The first man that was born in the world was a persecutor, namely Cain; and he hath a numerous offspring. Nero, Trajan, Domitian, Diocletian, Maximinus. Chrysostom saith, that the apples of his eyes fell out. Felix, earl of Wartenberg, being at supper at Augsburg, did take an oath, that before he died, he would ride up to the spurs in the blood of the Lutherans; but was afterwards choked in his own blood. Persecutors are the curse of the creation, being some of those 'thorns and briers' which the earth brings forth.

(2) Men are violent *in pursuing evil*.

(i) They are violent in *their opinions*: 'Privily they shall bring in damnable heresies, denying the Lord that bought them' (2 Pet. 2:1). Arius was such a one, and afterwards his bowels gushed out. And truly the spirit of Arius is yet alive at this day, while men dare deny the deity of the blessed Son of God. Many of the heretics of old were so violent, that their opinion was to them a Bible, and some of them died in maintaining their heresies. These were the devil's martyrs.

(ii) They are violent in *their passions*. Anger is a short frenzy. 'The tongue is a fire, a world of iniquity' (James 3:6). In this little member there is a great world, *viz.* a 'world of sin' (John 16:8). Such as would be counted sober, yet are drunk with passion. Their prayers are cold, but their anger hot. They spit fire as the serpent doth poison. Fiery passions without repentance bring men to the fiery furnace.

(iii) They are violent for *their lusts:* 'Serving divers lusts' (Titus 3:3). Lust is an inordinate desire or impulse, provoking the soul to the gratifying its carnal desires. Aristotle calls them brutish lusts, because when lusts are violent, they will not let reason or conscience be heard, but a man is carried brutishly to the satisfying of the flesh.

[1] Men are violent for their *drunken* lusts. Though death be in the cup, they will drink it off. One having almost lost his eyesight, the physician told him there was no cure for him, unless he would leave off his excessive drinking. Then saith he, 'Farewell sweet light.' He would rather lose his eyesight than leave his drinking.

[2] They are violent for their *unclean* lusts. Men are said to 'burn in lusts' (Rom. 1:27). The apostle intimateth that lust is a kind of fever. Feverish heats are not more pernicious to the body, than lust is to the soul. Oh what folly is it for a drop of pleasure to drink a sea of wrath!

[3] They are violent for their *oppressive* lusts, who wrong and defraud others and by violence take away their rights. Instead of clothing the naked, they make them who are clothed naked. These birds of prey live upon rapine. They are cruel, as if with Romulus they had been suckled with

OR, THE CHRISTIAN SOLDIER

the milk of wolves. They smile at the curses of the poor, and grow fat with their tears. They have forgotten Christ's caveat, 'Do violence to no man' (Luke 3:14). Ahab violently took away Naboth's vineyard (1 Kings 21:16). Hell is taken by this violence, 'who drink the wine of violence' (Prov. 4:17). This wine will turn to poison at last. 'Him that loveth violence God's soul hates' (Psa. 11:5).

[4] They are violent for their *covetous* lusts. Covetousness is the soul's dropsy, 'who pant after the dust of the earth' (Amos 2:7). They compass sea and land to make money their proselyte. Their god is made of gold, and to it they bow down. Those who bowed down on their knees to drink of the waters, were accounted unfit soldiers for Gideon (Judg. 7:6). So are those unfit for Christ, that stoop immoderately to the care of earthly things. They who are violent for the world, what have they but the wind? 'What profit hath he who hath laboured for the wind?' (Eccles. 5:16). The world cannot enrich the soul, it cannot remove pain. If pangs of conscience come, the world can no more give comfort, than a crown of gold can cure the headache.

4. A Reproof to *Backsliders and Apostates.*

(1) It reproves them *who have in part left off that holy strictness and violence in religion as once they had.* Their fervour is cooled and abated. What they do is so little that it cannot be called violence. They serve God, but are not fervent in spirit. They do not leave off duty, but they grow dead in duty. They have 'left their first love' (Rev. 2:4). It is with them as fire when it is going out; or as, the sun when it is going down. Like feverish men, before they were in a paroxysm, or hot fit of zeal; but now the cold fit hath

taken them; they are formal and frozen in religion. Time was when they 'called the sabbath a delight' (Isa. 58:13). How were their hearts raised in duty! How diligently did they seek him whom their soul loved! But now the case is altered; their religion doth languish, and even vanish. Time was when they were in an agony, and did send forth strong cries in prayer. Now the chariot wheels are pulled off, and the spirit of prayer is much abated. Their prayers do even freeze between their lips; a clear sign of the decay of grace. These persons are grown both lethargical and consumptive.

(i) *Lethargical.* 'I sleep, but my heart wakes' (Song of Sol. 5:2). Though grace was alive in her, 'her heart waked'; yet she was in a dull drowsy temper, 'I sleep.' When the heart burns in sin, and cools in duty, it is a sure sign of growing to a stupid lethargy.

(ii) *Consumptive.* There are two signs of persons in a spiritual consumption.

[1] When their desire after Christ and heaven is *not so strong as it was*. A consumptive man's stomach decays. Christians have not such violent affections to heavenly things: they can desire corn and wine, and the luscious delights of the earth; but Christ is less precious; they are not in pangs of desire after him. This is a sad symptom their grace is in a consumption.

[2] When they are *not so vigorous in motion*. A man that is lively and stirring at his work – it is a sign he is in health. But when he is listless, and cares not to stir, or put his hand to anything – this is a sign nature is declining. So when men have no heart to that which is good, they care not to put themselves upon the exercises of religion; they have lost a

spirit of activity for God; they serve him in a faint sickly manner; this is a sign they are consumptive.

When the pulse can scarce be felt – it beats so low – men are near dying. So when those who were once violent for heaven but now we can scarce perceive any good in them, the pulse beats low, grace is 'ready to die' (Rev. 3:2).

To you who have abated in your holy violence and are grown remiss in duty, let me expostulate with you, as the Lord did by the prophet Jeremiah: 'What iniquity have your fathers found in me?' (Jer. 2:5). What evil have you found in God, that you leave off your former strictness? Hath not God fed you with manna from above, and given you his Holy Spirit to be your guide and comforter? Hath he not made you swim in a sea of mercy? What evil have you found in prayer that you are less violent in it? Have not you had sweet intercourse with God? Have not you sometimes been melted and enlarged, insomuch that you have thought yourselves in the suburbs of heaven when you have been upon this mount? Hath not the dove of prayer brought an olive branch of peace in its mouth? What evil have you found in the word? There was a time when you did take this book and eat it, and it was honey in your mouth. Hath the word less virtue in it now? Are the promises like Aaron's dry rod, withered and sapless? What iniquity have you found in the ways of God, that you have abated your former violence in religion? 'O remember whence you are fallen, and repent, and do your first works' (Rev. 2:5). Consider seriously:

[i] *The less violence for heaven, the less peace.* Our consciences are never at peace in a drowsy state. It is the lively acting of grace that makes the heart calm and serene. These two go together, walking 'in the fear of God' and 'in

the comfort of the Holy Ghost' (Acts 9:31). Christian, if once thou growest remiss in religion, conscience will chide. If thou belongest to God, he will never let thee be quiet, but will send some affliction or other to awaken thee out of thy security, and make thee recover that active, lively frame of heart as once thou hadst.

[ii] You that grow more dead in God's service, and leave your first love, *give great advantage to Satan.* The less violent you are, the more violent he is; the less you pray, the more he tempts. And what a case are you now in! How can grace that is weak and sickly withstand violent temptations? Hence it is God who suffers his own people sometimes to fall into sin, as a just punishment of their lukewarmness, and to make them more zealous and violent for the future.

[iii] Your remissness in religion, though it may not damn you, *it will damage you.* You will lose that degree of glory which else you might have had. Though your remissness may not lose your crown, it will lessen it, and make it weigh lighter.

[iv] The more lazy a Christian's desires are, *the more lively his corruptions.* The weaker the body grows, the stronger the disease grows. Oh, therefore, pray for quickening grace (Psa. 143:11). Beg fresh gales of the Spirit to blow upon you. Never leave till you have recovered that holy violence which once you had.

(2) It reproves *those who have quite left off all violence:* they have left off reading and praying in their family. There is not so much as a face of religion to be seen, they are fallen finally. Such were Joash, Jehu, Julian. The goodly building of their profession which others admired, now hath not one stone left upon another.

But why do men thus run retrograde in their motion, and quite throw off that violence which they seemed once to have?

(i) Because *they never had a principle of spiritual life.* Things that move from a principle of life are constant, as the motion of the pulse; but things artificial are apt to be at a stand, and their motion ceases. As a clock when the weights are hung on, goes, but take out the weights and it stands. So the apostate never moved in religion but for gain and applause; and when these weights are taken off, he is at a stand, he goes no further. That branch must needs wither that hath no root to grow upon.

(ii) Men throw off all violence, and degenerate into apostasy, because *they never did duties of religion with delight.* St Paul 'delighted in the law of God in the inward man' (Rom. 7:22). It was his heaven to serve God. A man that delights in pleasure will never give over: but the apostate never had any true delight in the ways of God; he was rather forced with fear, than drawn with love: he served a master that he never cared for; no wonder then he leaves his service.

(iii) Men degenerate into apostasy through *unbelief.* 'They believed not in God … They turned back and tempted God (Psa. 78:22, 41). Sinners have jealous thoughts of God, they distrust his love, and therefore desert his service: they think they may pray, and hear, and to no purpose. 'What profit is it that we have kept his ordinances?' (Mal. 3:14). We may draw near to God in duty, but he will never draw near to us in mercy. Thus unbelief and atheism prevailing, the livery of religion is presently thrown off, and all former violence for heaven ceases. Infidelity is the mother of apostasy.

(iv) Men leave off their former violence, and prove Judases and devils because they *love something else more than religion.* There is some lust or other their heart is engaged to, and their violence for sin hath destroyed their violence for religion. Suleiman, the great Turk, seeing many Christians go over to Turkism, he asked them what moved them to turn Turks? They replied, they did it to be eased of their taxes. They were drawn from God through the prevalency of covetousness. If there be any lust in the heart predominant, it will get head, and destroy all former zeal for religion. Abimelech, a bastard, destroyed 'threescore and ten of his brethren upon one stone' (Judg. 9:5). If there be any lust the heart runs after, this bastard-sin will destroy threescore and ten duties; it will murder all that violence for heaven which a man did once seem to have.

(v) Men leave off former violence out of *pusillanimity:* if they are violent in religion, they fear they may lose their profits and preferments; nay, their lives. The coward never yet won the field. When carnal fear grows violent, all violence for heaven is at an end.

Incipit esse malus, qui timet esse bonus.[1]

Many of the Jews who were great followers of Christ, when they saw the swords and staves, left him. 'In the fear of man there is a snare' (Prov. 29:25). Carnal fear makes sin appear less than it is, but its danger is greater.

(vi) Men leave off violence for heaven for *want of patience*. Sensible feeling of joy is withheld, and they have not patience to stay for the full recompense of reward. Hypocrites are all for present pay; and if they have not that suddenly which they desire, they bid *adieu* to religion, and say as that wicked king, 'Why should I wait for the Lord any

[1] [The man who is afraid to be good, begins to be bad.]

longer?' (2 Kings 6:33). They consider not that God is a free agent, and will dispense his blessings in the fittest season, but they go to tie God up to their time. They forget that joy is a part of the reward, and would they have the reward and their work not yet finished? Doth the servant use to receive his pay before his work is done? 'The husbandman waits for the precious fruits of the earth': he doth not look to sow and reap in a day (James 5:7). But hypocrites are always in haste. They would reap joy before they have done sowing the seed of repentance. And because comfort is a while deferred, they are offended, and they will serve God no longer. Their patience is at an end, therefore their violence is at an end.

(vii) Men leave off holy violence and degenerate into profaneness *out of a just judgment of God, leaving them to themselves*. They oft resisted the Spirit, and sent it away sad from them, and now as a just judgment, God saith, 'My Spirit shall no longer strive.' And if this wind doth not blow upon their sails, they cannot move. If this sun withdraw from their climate, they must needs freeze in impenitency. They before sinned against clear convictions; they silenced conscience, and God hath seared it. And now if an angel should preach to them from heaven, it would do them no good. Oh how dismal is this! The thoughts of it may strike us into a holy consternation. Thus we see why men apostatize and leave off their violence for heaven.

Well, but what do they get by this? Let us see what a purchase apostates make.

They proclaim their folly; for all their former violence for heaven is lost. He who runs half the race and then faints, loseth the garland. 'When the righteous turneth away from his righteousness, all his righteousness that he hath done shall not be mentioned' (Ezek. 18:24). All men's prayers and tears are lost. The apostate unravels all that he hath been doing. He is like a man that with a pencil draws a curious picture, and then comes with his sponge and wipes it out again. 'Have ye suffered so many things in vain?' (Gal. 3:4). Perhaps for religion a man hath suffered many a reproach and affront; and have ye suffered all this in vain? Here is folly indeed.

It will be bitterness in the end. 'Know therefore that it is an evil and bitter thing that thou hast forsaken the Lord' (Jer. 2:19). Men, by leaving off their violence for heaven, get a thorn in their conscience, a blot in their name, a curse in their souls. What got Judas by his apostasy but a halter. So it will be bitterness in the end. The apostate when he dies, drops as a windfall into the devil's mouth.

5. It reproves *those who put off this violence for the kingdom till old age*. When they are fit for no other work, then they will begin this. No man saith, I will learn my trade when I am old. It is imprudence for one to begin to work for heaven when he is past his labour. There is a night of sickness and death coming, and our Saviour saith, 'The night cometh when none can work' (John 9:4). Sure a man can put forth but little violence for heaven when old age and old sins are upon him. Besides, how unworthy and disingenuous is it, to give the devil the flower of youth, and God the dregs of old age! Therefore God rejected Cain's sacrifice, because it was stale before he brought it (Gen. 4:5). There is little hope of their salvation who are never violent for heaven till their disease grows violent.

OR, THE CHRISTIAN SOLDIER

6. It reproves *those who are so far from using this violence for heaven, that they deride it.* These are your zealous ones. 'In the last days there shall be scoffers' (2 Pet. 3:3). Holy walking is become the object of derision: 'I am become the song of the drunkards' (Psa. 69:12). This shows a vile heart. There are some, who though they have no goodness themselves, yet honour them who are good. Herod reverenced John Baptist. But what devils are they who scoff at goodness, and reproach others for doing that which God commands! This age produceth such as sit in the chair of scorners, and throw their squibs at religion. In Bohemia, when some of the martyrs were the next day to suffer, they comforted themselves with this, that this was their last supper, and tomorrow they should feast with Christ in heaven. A Papist standing by, asked them in a jeer, if Christ had any cooks in heaven to dress their supper?

Oh take heed of such an Ishmael spirit! It is a sign of a man given over to the devil. God 'scorneth the scorner' (Prov. 3:34); and sure he shall never live with God, whose company God scorns.

7. It reproves *them who instead of taking heaven by force keep it off by force;* as if they were afraid of being happy, or as if a crown of glory would hurt them. Such are,

(1) The *ignorant,* who shut their eyes against the light, and refuse to be taught the way to heaven. 'Thou hast rejected knowledge' (Hos. 4:6). The Hebrew word signifies to reject with disdain. As I have read of a Scottish bishop, who thanked God he never knew what the Old and New Testament was. I wonder where the bishop took his text.

(2) The *profane,* who hate to be admonished, and had rather die than reform. 'They hate him that rebuketh

[73]

in the gate' (Amos 5:10). These keep off heaven by force. Such were those, 'Seeing you put away the word from you' (Acts 13:46). The Greek word may be rendered, seeing you push it away with your shoulders. As if a sick man should bolt out the physician, lest he should cure him: 'Who say unto the Almighty, depart from us' (Job 21:14). God is loath to be gone; he woos and beseeches sinners to accept of terms of mercy; he is loath to be gone. But sinners will have him gone. They say to him, Depart. May not we say to these, *Quis effascinavit?* 'Who hath bewitched you?' What madness beyond hyperbole is this, that you should not only forsake mercy, but fight against it; as if there were danger in going to heaven. These who put away salvation from them, are *felo de se*,[1] they do wilfully perish. They would not hear of anything that should save them. Were it not a sad epitaph to be written upon a man's tombstone, 'Here lies one that murdered himself'? This is the condition of desperate sinners, they keep off heaven by force, they are self-murderers. Therefore God writes their epitaph upon their grave: 'O Israel, thou hast destroyed thyself' (Hos. 13:9).

Questions for Self-examination

LET us then examine whether we put forth this holy violence for heaven? What is an empty profession without this? Like a lamp without oil. Let us all ask ourselves, what violence do we use for heaven?

1. *Do we strive with our hearts to get them into a holy frame?* How did David awaken all the powers of his soul to serve God? 'I myself will awake early' (Psa. 57:8). The heart is like a bell that is a long while a-raising.

[1] [A suicide.]

2. *Do we set time apart to call ourselves to account, and try our evidences for heaven?* 'My spirit made diligent search' (Psa. 77:6). Do we take our hearts as a watch all in pieces, to see what is amiss, and mend it? Are we curiously inquisitive into the state of our souls? Are we afraid of painted grace, as of painted happiness?

3. *Do we use violence in prayer?* Is there fire in our sacrifice? Doth the wind of the Spirit filling our sails, cause 'groans unutterable' (Rom. 8:26)? Do we pray in the morning as if we were to die at night?

4. *Do we thirst for the living God?* Are our souls big with holy desires? 'There is none upon earth my soul desires beside thee' (Psa. 73:25). Do we desire holiness as well as heaven? Do we desire as much to look like Christ, as to live with Christ? Is our desire constant? Is this spiritual pulse ever beating?

5. *Are we skilled in self-denial?* Can we deny our ease, our aims, our interest? Can we cross our own will to fulfil God's? Can we behead our beloved sin? To pluck out the right eye requires violence.

6. *Are we lovers of God?* It is not how much we do, but how much we love. Doth love command the castle of our hearts? Doth Christ's beauty and sweetness constrain us (2 Cor. 5:14)? Do we love God more than we fear hell?

7. *Do we keep our spiritual watch?* Do we set spies in every place, watching our thoughts, our eyes, our tongues? When we have prayed against sin, do we watch against temptation? The Jews, having sealed the stone of Christ's sepulchre, 'set a watch' (Matt. 27:66). After we have been at the word, or sacrament (that sealing ordinance), do we set a watch?

8. *Do we press after further degrees of sanctity?* 'Reaching forth unto those things which are before' (Phil. 3:13). A good Christian is a wonder. He is the most contented, yet the least satisfied. He is contented with a little of the world, but not satisfied with a little grace. He would still have more faith, and be anointed with fresh oil. Paul desired to 'attain unto the resurrection of the dead' (Phil. 3:11); that is, he endeavoured, if possible, to arrive at such a measure of grace as the saints shall have at the resurrection.

9. *Is there a holy emulation in us?* Do we labour to outshine others in religion? To be more eminent for love and good works? Do we something which is singular? 'What do you more than others?' (Matt. 5:47).

10. *Are we got above the world?* Though we walk on earth, do we trade in heaven? Can we say as David, 'I am still with thee' (Psa. 139:18). This requires violence, for motions upward are usually violent.

11. *Do we set ourselves always under God's eye?* 'I have set the Lord always before me' (Psa. 16:8)? Do we live soberly and godly, remembering whatever we are doing, our Judge looks on?

If it be thus with us, we are happy persons. This is the holy violence the text speaks of, and is the right way of taking the kingdom of God. And surely never did Noah so willingly put forth his hand to receive the dove into the ark, as Jesus Christ will put forth his hand to receive us into heaven.

It exhorts all Christians to this holy violence for heaven.

Objections to this Duty

But before I press the exhortation, let me remove some objections that may be made against this blessed violence.

1. *But we have no power of ourselves to save ourselves. You bid us be violent, as if you should bid a man tied fast in fetters to walk.*

It is true, we cannot till grace come, effectually operate to our own salvation. Before conversion we are purely passive; and when God bids us convert and turn, this is to show us what we ought to do, not what we can do. Yet let us do what we are able.

(1) *We have power to avoid those rocks which will certainly ruin our souls* – I mean *gross sins*. A man needs not be in bad company; he needs not swear, or tell a lie; nor would he do it if it were by law, death to swear an oath.

(2) *We have power to put ourselves upon the use of means, praying, reading, holy conference.* This will condemn men at the last day. They do not act so vigorously in their sphere as they might. They do not use the means, and try whether God will give grace. God will come with that soliciting question at last: 'Why didst not thou put my money to the exchangers?' (Matt. 25:27). Why didst not thou improve that power I gave thee?

Though we have not power to save ourselves, yet we must pursue after salvation, because God hath made a promise of grace, as well as to grace.

He hath promised to circumcise our hearts; to put his Spirit within us; to enable us to walk in his statutes (Ezek. 36:27). So that by prayer we are to put the bond in suit, and to press God with his own promise. Though I will not say with the Arminians, upon our endeavour God is bound to give grace. Yet he is not wanting to them that seek his grace. Nay, he denies his grace to none but them that wilfully refuse it: 'Israel would none of me' (Psa. 81:11).

2. *But this offering violence is hard, and I shall never be able to go through it.*

Admit it to be hard, yet it is a duty, and there is no disputing duty. God hath made the way to heaven hard.

(1) *To try our obedience.* A child obeys his father, though he commands him hard things. Peter's obedience and love was tried when Christ bade him come to him upon the water.

(2) *God doth it that he may raise the price of heavenly things.* Were the kingdom of glory easily obtained, we should not have valued it to its worth. Such is our nature, that we slight things which are easily come by. If pearls were common, they would soon fall in their price. If Christ and heaven might be had without violence, these blessings of the first magnitude would not have been had in such high veneration.

But let not the difficulty be objected. What though salvation-work be hard: (i) *Is it not harder to lay in hell?* Is not suffering vengeance worse than offering violence? (ii) *We do not argue so in other things.* An estate is hard to come by, therefore we will sit still: no, difficulty doth the more whet and sharpen our endeavour. And if we take such pains for these inferior things, how should we for that which is more noble and sublime! The profit will abundantly countervail the labour. (iii) Though the business of religion at first seems hard, *yet when once we are entered into it, it is pleasant.* When the wheels of the soul are oiled with grace, now a Christian moves in religion with facility and delight: 'I delight in the law of God in the inward man' (Rom. 7:22). Christ's yoke at the first putting on seems heavy; but when once it is on, it is easy. To serve God, to love God, to enjoy God, is the sweetest freedom in the world. The poets say, the top of Olympus is always quiet. The first climbing up the rocky hill of heaven is hard to flesh and blood, but when we are gotten up towards the top, there is peace and delight. We see a pleasant prospect, and are ready to cry out as Peter on the Mount of Transfiguration, 'It is good to be here.' What hidden manna do we now find! This is the anticipation or foretaste of glory.

3. But if I put myself upon this violent exercise in religion, then I shall lose that pleasure I have in my sin, my mirth and melody, and I shall exchange delight for labour; and so I shall be no more Naomi, but Marah. Voluptuous persons speak as the fig tree in the parable: 'Shall I leave my fatness and sweetness' (Judg. 9:11), all my former pleasures, and now offer violence to heaven, live a strict mortified life? This crosseth the stream of corrupt nature.

(1) *Leave the pleasure in sin.* The Scripture doth so describe sin, that one would think there should be little pleasure in it.

(i) The Scripture calls it a *debt*. Sin is compared to a debt of 'ten thousand talents' (Matt. 18:24). A talent of gold among the Hebrews, was valued at almost four thousand pounds. Ten thousand talents is a figurative speech, to express how great a debt sin is. And do you call this a pleasure? Is it any pleasure for a man to be in debt?

(ii) The Scripture calls sin a *disease:* 'The whole head is sick' (Isa. 1:5). Is it any pleasure to be sick? Though all do not feel this sickness, yet the less the distemper is felt, the more mortal.

(iii) The Scripture compares sin to *gall and wormwood* (Deut. 29:18). It breeds a bitter worm in the conscience. What a worm did Spira[1] feel! Sin stings a man with wrath (John 3:36). And do you call this a pleasure? Sure you 'put bitter for sweet' (Isa. 5:20)!

The pleasures of sin do gratify only the sensitive part of man, not the rational. Pleasures are called carnal, because they delight only the body. How absurd was that speech of the rich man in the gospel, when he was speaking of his store of goods, and his barns being full: 'Soul, take thine ease' (Luke 12:19). He might have said more properly, 'Body, take thine ease'; for his soul was never the better for his riches, nor could he feel any delight in them. Though his barns were full, his soul was empty. Therefore when Satan tells thee, 'If thou useth violence for heaven, thou wilt lose all thy pleasures'; ask him, 'What pleasures are they, Satan? Such as please only the senses, they do not delight the mind; they do not comfort the conscience; they are such delights wherein the brute creatures do exceed me.'

(iv) These sugared pleasures in sin the Scripture saith *are but for a season* (Heb. 11:25), like fire in straw, which

---

[1] [An eminent lawyer living near Venice in the Reformation period (16th century). He turned from Romanism, accepted the Protestant faith, but later apostatized and died in despair in 1548. His Life was published in Geneva in 1550, John Calvin supplying a preface. John Bunyan was deeply impressed by what happened to Spira. The man in the iron cage in the Interpreter's House in The Pilgrim's Progress undoubtedly represents him.]

makes a blaze, but is presently out: 'The world passeth away, and the lusts thereof' (1 John 2:17). It passeth away swiftly as a ship under sail. Worldly pleasures perish in the using – like a flying shadow, or flash of lightning. And are these to be preferred before an eternal weight of glory?

(v) The present sweetness which is in sin *will turn to bitterness at last.* Like the book the prophet ate, 'sweet in the mouth, but bitter in the belly' (Ezek. 3:3; Rev. 10:9). Honey is sweet, but it turns to gall. Sin is a sweet poison, it delights the pallet, but torments the bowels. When once the sinner's eyes come to be opened at death, and he feels some sparks of God's wrath in his conscience, then he will cry out for horror, and be ready to lay violent hands upon himself. We may say of the pleasures of sin, as Solomon of wine, 'Look not on the wine when it is red, when it shows its colour in the glass, afterwards it bites like a serpent' (Prov. 23:32). So look not on the smiling pleasures of sin; be not delighted with its beauty, but affrighted with its sting! Do the damned in hell feel any pleasure now in their sins? Hath their cup of wrath one drop of honey in it? Oh remember, after the golden crowns, and women's hair, come the lion's teeth (Rev. 9:7, 8). Thus I have answered the first part of the objection; 'I shall lose all my pleasures in sin.'

(2) *If I put forth this violence in religion, I shall exchange my delight for labour.* I must dig away through the rock; and while I work I must weep.

Though you must use violence, yet it is a *sweet violence;* it is a labour turned into delight: 'They shall sing in the ways of the Lord' (Psa. 138:5). To send out faith as a spy to view the heavenly Canaan, and pluck a bunch of grapes there – what delight is here! 'Joy in believing' (Rom. 15:13).

To love God, in whom all excellencies are combined, how sweet it is! To love beauty is delightful. To walk among the promises as among beds of spices, and taste the fruit, oh how pleasant! The labour of a Christian brings peace of conscience, and joy in the Holy Ghost.

Sed juvat ipse labor.[1]

And whereas it is said that this holy violence takes away our joy, and while we work we must weep; I answer, a Christian would not be without these tears. The tears of a saint (saith Bernard) have more true joy in them than all worldly delights. The oil of joy is for mourners (Isa. 61:3).

4. *I would use this violence for heaven, but I shall expose myself to the censure and scorn of others.* They will wonder to see me so altered, and think it nothing but a religious frenzy.

(1) *Consider who reproach thee;* they are the wicked; such as if Christ were alive on earth would reproach him. They are blinded by the god of this world (2 Cor. 4:4). It is as if a blind man should reproach a beautiful face.

(2) *What do they reproach thee for?* It is for offering violence to heaven. Is it a disgrace to be labouring for a kingdom? Tell them thou art doing the work that God hath set thee about. Better they should reproach thee for working in the vineyard, than God damn thee for not working.

(3) *Jesus Christ was reproached for thy sake:* 'He endured the shame of the cross' (Heb. 12:2). And wilt not thou be contented to bear reproaches for him? These are but the chips of the cross, which are rather to be despised than laid to heart.

---

[1] [But the very labour is joy.]

5. If I use this holy violence, and turn religious, then I shall lose such yearly profits which my sin hath brought in. As Amaziah said, 'What shall I do for the hundred talents?' (2 Chron. 25:9).

Is there any profit in sin? Did ever anyone thrive upon that trade? By the time you have cast up the reckoning, you will find but little profit.

(1) By the incomes that sin brings in, *thou treasurest up vengeance* (Rom. 2:5). While thou puttest unjust gain in the bag, God puts wrath in his vial. And will you call this profit? Whatever money a man gets in a sinful way, he must pay interest for it in hell.

(2) That cannot be for thy profit, which *makes thee come off a loser at last.* Thou loseth heaven and thy soul, and what can countervail this loss? 'What is a man profited if he gain the whole world, and lose his own soul?' (Matt. 16:26). God, saith Chrysostom, hath given a man two eyes; if he lose one, he hath another; but he hath but one soul, and if that be lost, he is undone forever.

6. But I have so much business in the world that I can find no time for this holy violence.

As the king of Macedon said, when they presented him with a book treating of happiness, 'I am not at leisure.'

See *the folly* of this objection: what is the main business of life, but looking after the soul? And for men to say they are so immersed in the world, that they cannot mind their souls, is most absurd and irrational. This is to make the greater give way to the lesser. As if a husbandman should say he is so busy in angling, or looking after his bees, that he hath no time to plough or sow. What is his occupation but ploughing? Such a madness is it to hear men say they are so taken up about the world, that they have no time for their souls.

Could God find time to think of thy salvation? Could Jesus Christ find time to come into the world, and be here above thirty years in carrying on this great design of thy redemption, and canst thou find no time to look after it? Is the getting a little money that which obstructs this violence for heaven? Thy money perish with thee!

Canst thou find time for thy body, time to eat and sleep, and not find time for thy soul? Canst thou find time to employ about thy recreation, and no time to employ about thy salvation? Canst thou find time for idle visits, and no time to visit the throne of grace?

Oh take heed thou goest not to hell in the crowd of worldly business! Joshua, who was a commander of an army, yet his work as a soldier was not to hinder his work as a Christian: he must pray as well as fight; and take the book of the law in his hand, as well as the sword (Josh. 1:8).

Thou, whosoever thou art that makest this objection about worldly business, let me ask thee, dost thou think in thy conscience that this will be a good excuse at the last day, when God shall ask thee, 'Why didst thou not take pains for heaven?' Thou shalt say, 'Lord, I was so steeped in worldly business, that I was hindered.' Were it a good plea for a servant to say to his master, he was so drunk that he could not work? Truly, it is much like thine, to say, thou were so drunk with the cares of the world that thou couldest not be violent for the kingdom.

Having answered these objections, *let me reassume the exhortation,* pressing all Christians to this violence for the

OR, THE CHRISTIAN SOLDIER

heavenly kingdom. As David's three worthies ventured their lives, and brake through the host of the Philistines for water (2 Sam. 23:16), such a kind of violence must we use, breaking through all dangers for obtaining the water of life.

Further Exhortations

1. *Consider the deplorable condition we are in by nature – a state of misery and damnation. Therefore what violence should we use to get out of it!* Were one plunged into quicksands, would he not use violence to get out? Sin is a quicksand, and is it not wisdom to extricate ourselves out? David being encompassed with enemies, said, 'His soul was among lions' (Psa. 57:4). It is true in a spiritual sense, our soul is among lions. Every sin is a lion that would devour us, and if we are in the lion's den, shall we not use violence to get out? The angels used violence to Lot. They laid hold on him, and pulled him out of Sodom (Gen. 19:16). Such violence must be used to get out of the spiritual Sodom. It is no safety to stay in the enemy's quarters.

2. *It is possible that in the use of means we may arrive at happiness.* Impossibility destroys endeavour. But here is a door of hope opened. The thing is feasible. It is not with us as with the damned in hell – there is a tombstone rolled over them. But while we are under the sound of Aaron's bell, and the silver trumpet of the gospel is blown in our ears, while the Spirit of grace breathes on us, and we are on this side of the grave, there is great hope that by holy violence we may win Paradise. An absolute impossibility of salvation is only for them who have sinned the sin against the Holy Ghost and cannot repent. But who these are is a secret sealed up

in God's book. Else here is great encouragement to all to be serious and earnest in the matters of eternity, because they are yet in a capacity of mercy, no final sentence is already passed. God hath not yet taken up the drawbridge of mercy. Though the gate of Paradise is strait, yet it is not shut. This should be as oil to the wheels to make us lively and active in the business of salvation. Therefore as the husbandman ploughs in hope (James 5:7), so we should pray in hope, do all our work for heaven in hope, for the white flag of mercy is yet held forth. So long as there was corn to be had in Egypt, the sons of Jacob would not sit starving at home (Gen. 42:3). So there is a kingdom to be obtained; therefore let us not sit starving in our sins any longer.

3. This violence for heaven *is the grand business of our lives*. What did we come into the world for else? We did not come hither only to eat and drink, and wear fine clothes. The end of our living is to be violent for the kingdom of glory. Should the body only be tended, this were to trim the scabbard, and let the blade rust; to preserve the lumber, and let the child be burnt. God sends us into the world as a merchant sends his factor to trade for him beyond the seas. So God sends us hither to follow a spiritual trade, to serve him and save our souls. If we spend all our time *aut aliud agendo, aut nihil*,[1] in dressing and pampering our bodies, or idle visits, we shall give but a sad account to God, when he shall send us a letter of summons by death, and bid us give an account of our stewardship. Were not he much to be blamed that should have a great deal of timber given him to build him a house, and he should cut out all this brave timber into chips? Just so is the case of many. God

[1] [Either doing something else, or doing nothing.]

gives them precious time in which they are to provide for a kingdom, and they waste this time of life, and cut it out all into chips. Let this excite violence in the things of God. It is the main errand of our living here. Shall we go out of the world and forget our errand?

4. *How violent are the wicked in ways of sin!* Violent for their *malicious* lusts: 'Their feet run to evil' (Prov. 1:16). Violent for their *unclean* lusts. Amnon offered violence to his sister; he would have his lust, though it cost him his life. Sinners tire out themselves in the devil's drudgery: 'They weary themselves to commit iniquity' (Jer. 9:5). They are out of breath with sin, yet not out of love with sin: 'They are mad upon their idols' (Jer. 50:38). So violent were the Jews, that they would spare no cost in their idolatrous worship: 'They lavish gold out of the bag' (Isa. 46:6). So fiercely were they bent upon idolatry, that they would sacrifice their sons and daughters to their idol gods: 'They built the high places of Baal to cause their sons and daughters to pass through the fire' (Jer. 32:35). Were men thus violent for their lusts and idols, and shall not we be violent for a kingdom? Nay, you that are now ingrafted into Christ, how violent perhaps have some of you been formerly in evil! How did you once spend yourselves in a sinful way, like Paul, who before his conversion 'breathed out threatenings and slaughter against the disciples of the Lord' (Acts 9:1)! Perhaps you have been violent in drawing others to sin. You have been tempters to them. And perhaps some of them whom you have seduced to sin are now crying out to you in hell, and saying, They had never come there, if it had not been for your example. Should not the consideration of this humble you? Should

not this make you the more violent in religion, that you may bring some glory to God before you die? Should not you be as industrious to save souls, as you have been to damn them? Were you to live to the age of Methuselah, you could never do God service sufficient for the dishonour you have done to him.

5. *This holy violence hath much delight mingled with it.* 'All her ways are pleasantness' (Prov. 3:17). Though the way of religion hath thorns in it (in respect of persecution), yet it is full of roses, in respect of that inward peace and contentment that the soul finds in it. A man is violent at his recreation, but there is an inward delight he takes in it which sweetens that violence. St Paul made religion his recreation: 'I delight in the law of God after the inward man' (Rom. 7:22): in the Greek, *I take pleasure;* not only heaven itself is delightful, but the way thither. What ravishing delight hath a gracious soul in prayer! 'I will make them joyful in the house of prayer' (Isa. 56:7). What delight in holy contemplation! A Christian hath such illapses of the Spirit, and meets with such transfigurations of soul, that he thinks himself half in heaven. Serving of God is like gathering of spices, or flowers, wherein these is some labour, but the labour is recompensed with delight. The way of sin hath bitterness in it. The bears while they lick the honey, are stung with the bees. So while men are following their lusts, they have checks of conscience, which are a foretaste of hell. Better want[1] the honey, than have this sting. But the violence for heaven is spiced with such joy, that it is not labour, but pleasure.

[1] [That is, lack.]

OR, THE CHRISTIAN SOLDIER

6. This violence and activity of spirit in religion puts a lustre upon a Christian. The more excellent anything is, the more active. The sun is a glorious creature, as a giant 'it runs its race' (Psa. 19:5). Fire, the noblest element, sparkles vigorously. The angels are described with wings (Isa. 6:2), which is an emblem of their swift obedience. The more violent we are in religion, the more angelical we are.

7. How violent was Christ about our salvation! He was in an agony; he 'continued all night in prayer' (Luke 6:12). He wept, he fasted, he died a violent death, he rose violently out of the grave. Was Christ so violent for our salvation, and doth it not become us to be violent who are so nearly concerned in it? Christ's violence was not only satisfactory, but exemplary. It was not only to appease God, but to teach us. Christ was violent in dying, to teach us to be violent in believing.

8. This holy violence brings rest; motion tends to rest: 'There remaineth a rest for the people of God' (Heb. 4:9). Indeed, there is a motion which doth not tend to rest; they who are violent in a way of sin, shall never have rest: 'They rest not day and night' (Rev. 4:8). Such as are graceless, shall be restless. But the violence a Christian takes leads to rest. As the weary traveller sits down at night and rests himself: 'Return to thy rest, O my soul' (Psa. 116:7). Holy violence is like the flying of Noah's dove to the ark, where it found rest.

9. If we use what violence we are able, God will help us. 'It is God who worketh in you both to will and to do' (Phil. 2:13). The Spirit helps us in prayer, and so proportionably in all other duties of religion (Rom. 8:26). The promise encourageth, and the Spirit enableth. In all earthly races a

[89]

man runs in his own strength; but in the race to heaven we have the Spirit of God helping us; he not only gives us the crown, when we have done running, but he gives us legs to run. He gives exciting and assisting grace. The Spirit of God helping, makes our work easy. If another helps to carry a burden, it is less difficult. If the loadstone draw the iron, it is not hard for the iron to move. If the Spirit of God, as a divine loadstone, draw and move the heart in obedience, now the work goes on with more facility.

10. *This blessed violence in religion would be preventative of much sin.* While men are idle in the vineyard, they are a prey to every temptation. We do not sow our seed in fallow ground; but Satan doth sow most of his seed of temptation in hearts that lie fallow. When he sees persons unemployed, he will find them work to do. He will stir them up to one sin or other. 'While men slept, the enemy sowed tares' (Matt. 13:25). When Satan finds men in a drowsy condition, their sleeping time is his tempting time. But by holy violence we prevent the devil's design. We are so busied about salvation, that we have no leisure to listen to temptation. St Jerome gave his friend this advice: To be always well employed, that when Satan came with a temptation, he might find him working in the vineyard. When the bird is flying it is safe, when it sits still on the bough, then it is in danger of being shot. When a Christian sits still and is inactive, then the devil shoots him with his fiery darts.

11. *The folly of such as are violent for the world, but not for the kingdom above.* Alas, how insipid are all these things that we lay out our sweat and violence upon, they will not make us happy. King Solomon did as it were put all the

creatures into a limbeck,[1] and still out the quintessence of them, and 'behold all was vanity' (Eccles. 2:11).

(1) These earthly things that we so toil for, are *uncertain* (1 Tim. 6:17). It is uncertain whether we shall get them. All that are suitors to a virgin do not speed. All that come to a lottery have not a prize.

(2) They are *unsatisfactory*. Could men heap up silver as dust; had they as much as the devil promised Christ, 'all the kingdoms of the world, and the glory of them' (Matt. 4:8), yet they can no more fill the heart, than a drop of water can fill the cistern: 'What profit hath he that hath laboured for the wind?' (Eccles. 5:16).

(3) They are *transient*. Death feeds at the root. All worldly possessions are like a castle of snow in the sun; or like a posy of flowers which withers while we are smelling it. Oh what folly is it to put forth all one's violence for the world, which is but 'for a season,' and not for Christ and grace. As if a condemned man should be earnest to get his dinner, but never mind getting his pardon.

12. The next motive is in the text; *this violence is for a kingdom*. 'The kingdom of heaven suffereth violence.' And what will we be violent for, if not for a kingdom? Men will wade to a kingdom through blood: this is a kingdom worth striving for. Cyprus is an island so exceeding fertile and pleasant, that it was anciently called *Macaria,* which signifies *blessed*. This title of *blessed* may more fitly be given to the heavenly kingdom. If the mountains were gold, if every sand of the sea were a diamond, if the whole globe were a shining crysolite, it were infinitely beneath the glory of this kingdom.

[1] [A distilling apparatus.]

(1) The *immunities* of the heavenly kingdom are great.

(i) There shall be *freedom from sin*. Here sin keeps house with us. It is as natural to us to sin, as to breathe. The soul that is most refined and clarified by grace is not without some dregs of corruption. St Paul cried out of a 'body of sin' (Rom. 6:6; cf. Rom 7:24). He who is inoculated into Christ hath still a taste and relish of the wild olive. But when we ascend to the heavenly kingdom, this mantle of sin shall drop off. That kingdom is so pure, that it will not mix with any corruption (Rev. 21:27). A sinful thought shall not creep in there. There is beauty which is not stained with lust, and honour which is not swelled with pride.

(ii) In that blessed kingdom there shall be *freedom from the assaults of the red dragon*. It is sad to have Satan daily soliciting us by his temptations, and labouring to trepan[1] us into sin. Temptation is the devil's powder-plot, to blow up the fort-royale of our grace. But this is the blessed freedom of the heavenly kingdom: it is not capable of temptation. The old Serpent is cast out of Paradise.

(iii) In that blessed kingdom there shall be *freedom from divisions*. In this world God's own tribes go to war. Ephraim envies Judah, and Judah vexeth Ephraim. The soldier's spear pierced Christ's side; but the divisions of saints pierce his heart. Christ prayed that all his people might be one, as he and his Father are one (John 17:21). But how do Christians by their discords and animosities go about what in them lies to frustrate Christ's prayer! But in the kingdom of heaven there is perfect love, which, as it casts out fear, so strife. Those Christians that could not live quietly together here, in that kingdom shall be united. There Calvin and

[1] [To lure or ensnare.]

Luther are agreed. In that celestial kingdom there shall be no vilifying or slandering one another, or raking into those sores which Christ died to heal. Christians that could not pray together shall sing together in that glorious choir. There shall not be one jarring string in the saints' music.

(iv) In that heavenly kingdom there shall be *freedom from all molestations*. Our lives now are interlined with troubles: 'My life is spent with grief, and my years with sighing' (Psa. 31:10). There are many things to occasion disquiet: sometimes poverty afflicts; sometimes sickness tortures; sometimes unkindness of friends breaks the heart. Our lives, like the Irish seas, are full of tempests; but in the kingdom of heaven is nothing to administer grief. There all is serene and calm; nothing within to humble, or without to molest.

(2) The *royalties and excellencies* of that kingdom are great. We may say of heaven, as it was said of Laish, 'We have seen the land, and behold it is very good; a place where there is no want of any thing' (Judg. 18:9, 10).

(i) The heavenly kingdom *abounds with riches:* 'The twelve gates were twelve pearls' (Rev. 21:21). Earthly kingdoms are fain to traffic abroad for gold and spices: in the kingdom of God are all rarities to be had, all commodities of its own growth; therefore figured by the tree of life bearing several sorts of fruit (Rev. 22:2). How rich is that place where the blessed Deity shines forth in its immense glory infinitely beyond the comprehension of angels!

(ii) The *delights* of the heavenly kingdom are unmixed. The comforts here below are chequered. Honour may be stained with disgrace; joy interlarded with sorrow. Our stars are mixed with clouds; but the delicacies of heaven are pure as well as pleasant. There is honey that hath not one drop of gall. The crystal spring of joy hath no settling of sorrow at bottom. The rose in that paradise is without prickles; the sun in that horizon is without eclipse.

(iii) This kingdom above is *durable*. Suppose earthly kingdoms to be more glorious than they are, their foundations of gold, their walls of pearl, their windows of sapphire, yet they are corruptible: 'I will cause the kingdom to cease' (Hos. 1:4). Troy and Athens now lie buried in their own ruins. But the kingdom of glory, as it is made without hands, so without end. It is 'the everlasting kingdom' (2 Pet. 1:11).

Now methinks, if ever we will use violence, it should be for this kingdom. This kingdom will make amends for all our labour and pains. Caesar marching towards Rome, and hearing that all the people were fled from it, said, 'They that will not fight for this city, what city will they fight for?' So if we will not put forth violence for this kingdom of heaven, what will we be violent for? I say to all, as the children of Dan in another sense; 'We have seen the land, and behold it is very good; and are ye still? Be not slothful to go, and enter to possess the land' (Judg. 18:9).

13. *The more violence we have used for heaven, the sweeter heaven will be when we come there.* As when a man hath been grafting trees, or setting flowers in his garden, it is pleasant to review and look over his labours; so in heaven, when we shall remember our former zeal and activity for the kingdom, it will indulcorate[1] heaven, and add to the joy of it. For a Christian to think, 'Such a day I spent in examining my heart, such a day I was weeping for sin; when others

[1] [Sweeten.]

were at their sport, I was at my prayers: and now, have I lost anything by this violence? My tears are wiped away, and the wine of paradise cheers my heart. I now enjoy him whom my soul loves. I now have the crown and white robes I so longed for. Oh how pleasant will it be to think, This is the heaven my Saviour bled for, and I sweat for!'

14. *The more violence we put forth in religion, the greater measure of glory we shall have.* That there are degrees of glory in heaven, seems to me beyond dispute.

(1) There are degrees of *torment in hell;* therefore, by the rule of contraries, degrees of glory in heaven.

(2) The Scripture speaks of *'a prophet's reward'* (Matt. 10:41), which is a degree above others'.

(3) The saints are said to shine *'as the stars'* (Dan. 12:3). Now one star differeth from another in glory.

So there are gradations of happiness. And of this judgment is Calvin, as also many of the ancient fathers. Consider then seriously, the more violent we are for heaven, and the more work we do for God, the greater will be our reward. The hotter our zeal, the brighter our crown. Could we hear the blessed souls departed speaking to us from heaven, sure thus they would say, 'Were we to leave heaven awhile, and to dwell on the earth again, we would do God a thousand times more service than ever we have done. We would pray with more life, act with more zeal; for now we see, the more hath been our labour, the more astonishing is our joy, and the more flourishing our crown.'

15. *Upon our violence for the kingdom, God hath promised mercy*. 'Ask and it shall be given you; seek and ye shall find; knock, and it shall be opened to you' (Matt. 7:7).

(1) *Ask.* Ask with importunity. A faint asking begs a denial. King Ahasuerus stood with his golden sceptre, and said to Queen Esther, 'Ask, and it shall be given, to half of the kingdom.' But God saith more: Ask, and he will give the whole kingdom (Luke 12:32). It is observable, the door of the tabernacle was not of brass, but had a thin covering, a veil, that they might easily enter into it; so the door of heaven is, through Christ's blood, made easy, that our prayers put up in fervency may enter. Upon our asking, God hath promised to give his Spirit (Luke 11:13). And if he give his Spirit, he will give the kingdom. The Spirit first anoints (1 John 2:27), and after its anointing oil comes the crown.

(2) *Seek and ye shall find.* But is it not said, 'Many shall seek to enter in, and shall not be able' (Luke 13:24)? I answer, that is, because they did seek in a wrong manner.

(i) They did seek *ignorantly,* setting up an altar to an unknown god. It is ill seeking pearls in the dark. Ignorant people seek heaven by their good meanings; they seek in the dark, and no wonder they miss of salvation.

(ii) They did seek *proudly.* They sought heaven by their own merits, whereas we are to seek the kingdom in Christ's strength, and in his name.

(iii) They did seek *lazily;* as the spouse sought Christ on her bed, and found him not (Song of Sol. 3:1). So many seek Christ in a supine manner; they seek, but they do not strive.

(iv) They did seek *hypocritically;* they would have heaven and their lusts too. Like that Protestant prince Camden speaks of, who set up one altar in the same church to the true God, and another to the idol. But let not such seekers ever think to find happiness. Let them not think to lie in Delilah's lap, and go to Abraham's bosom when they die.

(v) They did seek *inconstantly:* because mercy did not come presently, they gave over seeking.

But else if we seek the kingdom of heaven cordially, God hath pawned his truth in a promise, we shall find: 'Then shall ye find me, when you search for me with all your heart' (Jer. 29:13).

(3) *Knock, and it shall be opened.* Knocking implies violence. But we must do as Peter; he 'continued knocking' (Acts 12:16). We must continue knocking by prayer, and heaven's gates shall be opened. How may this be as oil to the wheels! How may it excite holy violence, when we have so gracious a promise of mercy upon our earnest seeking of it!

16. *This holy violence will not hinder men in their secular employments.*

Violence for the kingdom, and diligence in a calling, are not inconsistent. Christians, you may work for heaven, yet work in a trade. God hath given you a body and a soul, and he hath allotted you time to provide for both. He hath given you a body, therefore be diligent in your calling; he hath given you a soul, therefore be violent for heaven. These two may well stand together, providing for a family, and praying in a family. He that doth not exercise himself in some honest employment, is guilty of the breach of that commandment, 'Six days shalt thou labour.' God never sealed warrants for idleness. The sluggard shall be indicted at the day of judgment for letting his field be over-run with thorns. They are hypocrites who talk of living by faith, but refuse to live in a calling. Only remember, that the pains you take in religion must exceed the other: 'Seek ye first the kingdom of God' (Matt. 6:33). First, in order of time, before all things; and first in order of affection, above all things. Your soul is the nobler part, therefore that must be chiefly looked after. In your calling show diligence; in religion violence.

But some may say, 'we are so incumbered in the world that all time for religion is swallowed up; we cannot get leave from our calling to read or pray.'

If your trade be such that you cannot allow yourselves time for your souls, then your trade is unlawful. There are two things make a trade unlawful. First, when persons deal in such commodities as they know cannot be used without sin. Selling of black-spots, or idolatrous pictures and crucifixes. Second, when their trade doth so involve them in worldly business that they cannot mind eternity, or make out one sally to the throne of grace. They are so much in the shop, that they cannot be in the closet.

If there be such a trade to be found, doubtless it is unlawful. But let not men lay it upon their trade, but upon themselves; their trade would give them leave to serve God, but their covetousness will not give them leave. Oh how many put a fallacy upon their own souls, and cheat themselves into hell.

17. *There is but a short space of time granted us, therefore work the harder for heaven before it be too late.* Indeed we are apt to dream of a long life, as if we were not sojourners, but natives, and were to stay here always. The blossom of childhood hopes to come to the budding of youth; and the bud of youth hopes to come to the flower of age; and the flower of age hopes to come to old age; and old age hopes to renew it's strength as the eagle. But if we measure life by a pair of scripture-compasses, it is very short. It is compared

to a 'flying shadow' (Job 8:9); to a 'handbreadth' (Psa. 39:5), as if there were but a span between the cradle and the grave – *parum abest a nihilo*.[1] – Is the time of life so short, and may be shorter than we are aware? What need is there zealously to improve it before it be slipped away? If time runs, let us 'so run' (1 Cor. 9:24). He that hath a great business in hand, and the time allotted for doing it is but short, had not need lose any of that time. A traveller that hath many miles to ride, and the night ready to approach, had need spur on the harder, that the night doth not overtake him. So we have a long journey and the night of death is drawing on. How should we use spurs to our sluggish hearts that we may go on more swiftly!

18. *A man's personal day of grace may be short.* There is a time while the sceptre of grace is held forth: 'Now is the accepted time' (2 Cor. 6:2). The Lord hath prefixed a time wherein the means of grace shall work or not work. If a person come not in by such a time, God may say, 'Never fruit grow on thee more.' A sign this day of grace is past, is when conscience hath done speaking, and God's Spirit hath done striving. Whether this day may be longer or shorter, we cannot tell; but because it may so soon expire, it is wisdom to take the present opportunity, and use all violence for heaven. The day of grace hastens away. No man can (like Joshua) bid this sun stand still. And if this critical day be once past, it cannot be recalled. The day of *grace* being lost, the next is a day of *wrath*. Jerusalem had 'a day,' but she lost it: 'If thou hadst known, even thou, in this thy day, the things which belong unto thy peace, but now they

---

[1] [It is little more than nothing.]

are hid from thine eyes' (Luke 19:42). After the expiration of the day of grace, no means or mercies shall prove effectual. Now 'they are hid from thine eyes' – which is like the ringing a doleful knell over a dying person. Therefore put forth all violence for heaven, and do it in this 'thy day,' before it be too late, and the decree be gone forth.

19. *If you neglect the offering violence now, there will be no help for you after death,* when men shall open their eyes in another world and see into what a damned condition they have sinned themselves. Oh now what would they not do, what violence would they not use, if there were a possibility they might be saved! When once the door of mercy is shut, if God would make new terms far harder than before, they would readily seal them. If God should say to the sinner after death:

'Wouldst thou be content to return to the earth, and live there under the harrow of persecution a thousand years for my sake?'

'Yes, Lord, I will subscribe to this, and endure, the world's fury, may I have but thy favour at last.'

'But, wilt thou be content to serve an apprenticeship in hell a thousand years, where thou shalt feel the worm gnawing, and the fire burning?'

'Yes, Lord, even in hell I submit to be; so that after a thousand years I may have a release, and that "bitter cup" may pass away from me.'

'But, wilt thou for every lie thou hast told, endure the rack; wilt thou for every oath that thou hast sworn, fill a bottle of tears; wilt thou for every sin thou hast committed, lie ten thousand years in sackcloth and ashes?'

'Yes Lord, all this and more if thou requirest, I will subscribe to; I am content now to use any violence, if I may but at last be admitted into thy kingdom.'

'No,' will God say, 'there shall be no such condition proposed to thee, no possibility of favour, but thou shalt be forever among the damned; and who is able to dwell with everlasting burnings?'

Oh, therefore be wise in time, now while God's terms are more easy, embrace Christ and heaven, for after death there will be nothing to be done for your souls. The sinner and the furnace shall never be parted.

20. *How without all apology will you be left, if you neglect this violence for heaven!* Methinks I hear God thus expostulating the case with sinners at the last day:

'Why did you not take pains for heaven? Hath there not been a prophet among you? Did not my ministers lift up their voice like a trumpet? Did not they warn you? Did not they persuade you to use this violence, telling you that your salvation depended upon it? But the most melting rhetoric of the gospel would not move you. Did I not give you time to look after your souls? "I gave her space to repent" (Rev. 2:21). Did not you promise in your vow in baptism, that you would take heaven by force, fighting under my banner against world, flesh, and devil? Why then did you not use violence for the kingdom? It must be either sloth or obstinacy. You could be violent for other things – for the world, for your lusts – but not for the kingdom of heaven. What can you say for yourselves, why the sentence of damnation should not pass?'

Oh how will men be confounded and left speechless at such a time, and God's justice shall be cleared in their condemnation, 'that thou mayest be clear when thou judgest' (Psa. 51:4)! Though the sinner shall drink a sea of wrath, yet not one drop of injustice.

21. *What a vexation it will be at the last to lose the kingdom of glory for want of a little violence!* When one shall think with himself: 'I did something in religion, but I was not violent enough. I prayed, but I should have brought fire to the sacrifice. I heard the word, but I should have received the truth in love. I humbled myself with fasting, but I should with humiliation have joined reformation. I gave Christ's poor good words; I did bid them be warmed, but I should have clothed and fed them. And for want of a little more violence I have lost the kingdom.'

The prophet bade the king of Israel smite upon the ground (2 Kings 13:18). And he 'smote thrice, and stayed, and the man of God was wroth, and said, Thou shouldest have smitten five or six times; then hadst thou smitten Syria till thou hadst consumed it' (verse 19). So a man doth something in religion, he smites thrice and then stays; whereas had he but put forth a little more violence for heaven he had been saved. What a mischief is this but to half do one's work, and by shooting short to lose the kingdom! Oh how will this cut a man to the heart when he is in hell, to think, 'Had I but gone a little further it had been better with me than it is now! I had not been thus tormented in the flame.'

22. *The examples of the saints of old, who have taken heaven by force.* David broke his sleep for meditation (Psa. 119:148). His violence for heaven was boiled up to zeal: 'My zeal hath consumed me' (Psa. 119:139). And St Paul did 'reach forth unto those things which were before' (Phil. 3:13).

The Greek word signifies to *stretch out the neck:* a metaphor taken from racers that strain every limb, and reach forward to lay hold upon the prize. We read of Anna, a prophetess, 'She departed not from the temple, but served God with fastings and prayers night and day' (Luke 2:37). How industrious was Calvin in the Lord's vineyard. When his friends persuaded him for his health's sake, to remit a little of his labours, saith he, 'Would ye have the Lord find me idle when he comes?' Luther spent three hours a day in prayer. It is said of holy Bradford,[1] preaching, reading and prayer was his whole life. 'I rejoice,' said Bishop Jewel 'that my body is exhausted in the labours of my holy calling.' How violent were the blessed martyrs! They wore their fetters as ornaments; they snatched up torments as crowns, and embraced the flames as cheerfully as Elijah did the fiery chariot that came to fetch him to heaven. 'Let racks, fires, pullies, and all manner of torments come, so I may win Christ,' said Ignatius. These pious souls resisted unto blood. How should these provoke our zeal! Write after these fair copies.

23. *If the saints with all their violence have much ado to get to heaven, how shall they come there who use no violence?* 'If the righteous scarcely be saved, where shall the ungodly and sinner appear?' (1 Pet. 4:18). If they that strive as in an agony can hardly get in at the strait gate, what shall become of them that never strive at all? If St Paul did 'keep under his body,' by prayer, watching, fasting (1 Cor. 9:27), how shall they be saved, that wholly let loose the reins to the flesh, and bathe themselves in the luscious streams of carnal pleasure?

[1] [John Bradford, English reformer and martyr.]

24. *This sweating for heaven is not to endure long.* 'After ye have suffered a while' (1 Pet. 5:10). So after ye have offered violence a while, there shall be an end put to it. Your labour shall expire with your life. It is but a while and you shall have done weeping, wrestling, praying; it is but a while and the race will be over, and you shall receive 'the end of your faith, the salvation of our souls' (1 Pet. 1:9). It is but a while and you shall have done your weary marches, you shall put off your armour, and put on white robes. How should this excite a spirit of holy violence! It is but a few months or days and you shall reap the sweet fruit of your obedience. The winter will be past, and the spring flowers of joy shall appear. Dr Taylor[1] comforted himself when he was going to the stake: 'I have but two stiles to go over, and I shall be at my Father's house.' Christians, you have but a little way to go, a little more violence, a few more tears shed, a few more sabbaths kept, and then your hopes shall be crowned with the beatifical sight of God. When the vapour is blown away, then we may see the sun clearly: so when this short vapour of life is blown away, then we shall behold Christ, the Sun of Righteousness, in all his glory. 'We shall see him as he is' (1 John 3:2).

25. *If you are not violent for heaven, you walk contrary to your own prayers.* You pray that God's will may be done by you on earth, 'as it is done in heaven' (Matt. 6:10). Now how is God's will done in heaven? Are not the angels swift in doing the will of God? Like the stars above the equinoctial that are moved many millions of miles in an hour. The seraphims are described with wings, to show how velocious

---

[1] [Rowland Taylor, English reformer and martyr.]

and winged they are in their obedience (Isa. 6:2). Now if you are not violent in your spiritual motion, you live in a contradiction to your own prayers. You are far from being as angels, you creep as snails in the way to heaven.

26. *This holy and blessed violence would make Christians willing to die.* What is it makes men so loath to die? They are as a tenant that is loath to go out of a house. Why so? Because their conscience accuseth them that they have taken little or no pains for heaven. They have been sleeping, when they should have been working, and now death looks ghastly; they are afraid death will carry them prisoners to hell. Whereas the Christian that hath been active in religion, and hath spent his time in the service of God, he can look death in the face with comfort. He who hath been violent for heaven in this life, need not fear a violent death. Death shall do him no hurt; it shall not be a destruction, but a deliverance: it shall purge out sin, and perfect glory. What made St Paul say, *Cupio dissolvi*, 'I desire to be dissolved' (Phil. 1:23)? Surely the reason was, he had been a man of violence; he did spend himself for Christ, and laboured more than all the other apostles (1 Cor. 15:10). And now he knew there was a crown laid up for him. Augustus the emperor did desire that he might have a quiet easy death. If anything make our pillow easy at death, and we go out of the world quietly, it will be this holy violence that we have put forth in the business of religion.

27. *If for all that hath been said, you will either sit still, or keep your sweat for something else than heaven, know, there is a time shortly coming when you will wish you had used this violence.* When sickness seizeth on you, and your disease

begins to grow violent, and you think God's sergeant is at the door, then what wishes will you make? 'Oh that I had been more violent for heaven! Oh that I had been praying when I was dancing and making merry! Oh that I had had a Bible in my hand when I had a pack of cards! How happy then might I have been! But alas, my case is miserable! What shall I do? I am so sick, that I cannot live, and so sinful, that I dare not die! Oh that God would respite me a little longer, that he would put a few more years in my lease, that a little space might be granted me to recover my lost hours!'

As one said on her death-bed, 'Call Time again';[1] but Time will not be called again. At the hour of death sinners will awake out of their lethargy, and fall into a frenzy of horror and despair. And shall not all these arguments prevail with men to be violent for the kingdom? What a hardened piece is a sinner's heart! We read that at Christ's passion 'the rocks rent' (Matt. 27:51). But nothing will move a sinner. The rocks will sooner rend than his heart. If all that I have said will not prevail, it is a sign ruin is towards: 'They hearkened not to the voice of their father, because the Lord would slay them' (1 Sam. 2:25).

A Necessary Cautionary Note

YET this caution I must necessarily insert, though we shall not obtain the kingdom *without* violence, yet not *for* our violence. When we have done all, look up to Christ and free grace. Bellarmine saith, we merit heaven *ex congruo*.[2] No, though we are saved in the use of means, yet by grace too:

---

[1] [Among the last words of Queen Elizabeth I.]
[2] [In accordance with our actions (on earth).]

'By grace ye are saved' (Eph. 2:5). Heaven is a donative: 'It is my Father's good pleasure to give you a kingdom' (Luke 12:32). Why may one say, '*I* have used violence for it, *I* have wrought for the kingdom'? *I*, but it is a gift that free grace bestows! We must look up to Christ for acceptance. Not our sweat, but his blood saves. Our labouring qualifies us for heaven, but Christ's dying purchased heaven. Alas, what is all that we can do in comparison of glory? What is the shedding of a tear to a crown? Therefore we must renounce all in point of justification, and let Christ and free grace carry away the glory of our salvation. God must help us in our working. 'It is God which worketh in you both to will and to do' (Phil. 2:13). How then can we merit by our working, when it is God that helps us in our working?

Rules and Directions for Getting this Violence for Heaven

I shall, in the next place, lay down some *rules* or *directions* how to get this blessed violence.

1. *Take heed of those things which will hinder this violence for heaven.*

(1) Take heed of *unbelief*. Unbelief is a great remora,[1] as it is discouraging. When a Christian is working for heaven, unbelief whispers thus, To what purpose is all this pains? I had as good sit still. I may pray, and not be heard; I may work, and have no reward; I may come near heaven, yet miss it. 'And they said, there is no hope' (Jer. 18:12). Unbelief destroys hope. And if you cut this sinew of religion, all violence for heaven ceaseth. Unbelief raiseth a cloud of

---

[1] [Hindrance or drag.]

despondency in the heart. Alas, you will never be able to go through the work of religion – so many precepts to obey, so many temptations to resist, so many afflictions to bear – that you will *succumbere oneri*, fall under the burden; you will tire in your march to heaven. Unbelief raiseth jealous thoughts of God, it represents him as an 'austere' master, and that if we fail in ever so little a punctilio, he will take the extremity of the law upon us. This discourageth the soul in the use of means. Unbelief doth as Sanballat and Tobiah did to the Jews: 'They made us afraid, saying, Their hands shall be weakened from the work' (Neh. 6:9). Oh take heed of unbelief, it destroys this holy violence. We read of Jeroboam's arm being withered (1 Kings 13:4). Unbelief withers the arm of the soul that it cannot stretch itself forth to any spiritual action. Unbelief doth the devil the greatest kindness. It makes way for his temptations to enter, which do so enchant and bewitch us that we cannot work. Beware of this sin. Believe the promises. God 'is good to the soul that seeks him' (Lam. 3:25). Do but seek him with importunity, and he will open both his heart and heaven to thee.

(2) Take heed of *puzzling your thoughts about election*. A Christian may think thus, 'What, should I take pains? Perhaps I am not elected, and then all my violence is to no purpose.' Thus, many are taken off from the use of means, and the business of religion is at a stand. Whereas no man can justly say he is not elected. It is true, some of God's children have said so in temptation; but as Peter at the Transfiguration said he knew not what, so these in a temptation. But no man can say on just grounds, he is not elected, unless he can prove that he hath sinned the sin against the Holy Ghost. For anyone to assert non-election is

a sin; for that which keeps him in sin, must needs be sinful. But this opinion keeps him in sin. It discourageth him from the use of means, and cuts the sinews of all endeavours. Do not therefore perplex your thoughts about election. This book is sealed, and no angel can unclasp it.

The rule Christians are to go by, is God's revealed will, not his secret. God's revealed will is that we should pray and repent; by this we make our calling sure; and by making our calling sure, we make our election sure. If I see the beds of spices grow and flourish, I know the sun hath been there. And if I find the fruits of obedience in my heart, I may conclude God's electing love hath shined upon me: 'God hath from the beginning chosen you to salvation through sanctification' (2 Thess. 2:13).

(3) Take heed of *too much violence after the world*. The world cools good affections. The earth puts out the fire. The world's silver trumpet sounds a retreat, and calls men off from their pursuit after heaven. The world hindered the young man from following Christ: 'he went away sorrowful.' Whereupon saith our Saviour, 'How hardly shall they that have riches enter into the kingdom of God!' (Luke 18:24). Demas's religion lay buried in the earth: 'Demas hath forsaken me, having loved this present world' (2 Tim. 4:10). It was a saying of Pius V: 'When I first entered into orders, I had some good hope of my salvation; when I became a cardinal, I doubted of it; but since I came to be Pope, I do even despair of it.' Jonathan pursued the victory till he came at the honeycomb, and then he stood still (1 Sam. 14:27). Many are violent for the kingdom of God, till gain or preferment offers itself. When they meet with this honey, then they stand still. The world blinds men's eyes that they

do not see the way, and fetters their feet that they do not run in the way of God's commandments. Mithridates, king of Pontus, being worsted by the Romans, and fearing he should not escape them, caused a great deal of silver and gold to be scattered in the ways, which while the Roman soldiers were busy ingathering, he got away from them. The like stratagem Satan useth. Knowing what tempting things riches are, he throws them in men's way, that while they are eager ingathering these, he may hinder them in their pursuit of happiness. I have observed some who did once, Jehu-like, drive on furiously in the cause of religion, when the world hath come in upon them their chariot-wheels have been pulled off, and they have driven on heavily. Were a man to climb up a steep rock, and had weights tied to his legs, they would hinder his ascent. Men's golden weights hinder them in climbing up this steep rock which leads to salvation. The world's music charms men asleep, and when they are asleep, they are not fit to work. A thing cannot be carried violently to two extremes at once. The ship cannot go full sail to the east and west at the same time. So a man cannot be violent for heaven and earth at once. He may have Christ and the world, but cannot love Christ and the world (1 John 2:15). He that is all fire for the world, will be all ice for heaven.

Take heed of engaging your affections too far in these secular things. Use the world as your servant, but do not follow it as your master.

(4) Take heed of *indulging any lust*. Sin lived in will spoil all violence for heaven. Sin enfeebles: it is like the cutting of Samson's hair, and then the strength departs. Sin is *aegritudo animi,* the soul's sickness. Sickness takes a man off his

legs, and doth so dispirit him, that he is unfit for any violent exercise. A sick man cannot run a race. Sin lived in takes a man quite off from duty, or makes him dead in it. The more lively the heart is in sin, the more dead it is in prayer. How can he be earnest with God for mercy whose heart accuseth him of secret sin? Guilt breeds fear; and that which strengthens fear, weakens violence. Adam having sinned, was afraid, and hid himself (Gen. 3:10). When Adam had lost his innocence, he lost his violence.

Therefore lay the axe to the root. Let sin be hewn down. Not only abstain from sin in the act, but let the love of sin be mortified, and let every sin be put to the sword. Many will leave all their sins but one; save one sin, and lose one soul. One sin is a fetter. A man may lose the race as well by having one fetter on his leg, as if he had more. I have read of a great monarch, that flying from his enemy, he threw away the crown of gold on his head, that he might run the faster. So that sin which thou didst wear as a crown of gold, throw it away that thou mayest the faster run to the heavenly kingdom.

(5) If you would be violent for heaven, take heed of *despondency of spirit*. Be serious, but cheerful. He whose spirit is pressed down with sadness, is unfit to go about his work. An uncheerful heart is unfit to pray, or praise God. When the strings of a lute are wet, it will not put forth any sweet harmony. Such as go drooping under fears and discouragements cannot be violent in religion. When a soldier faints in the field, he soon lets fall his sword. David chides himself out of his melancholy: 'Why art thou cast down, O my soul? why art thou disquieted within me? hope thou in God' (Psa. 43:5). A sad heart makes a dull action.

We use the drum and trumpet in battle that the noise of the trumpet may excite and quicken the soldiers' spirits, and make them fight more vigorously. Cheerfulness is like music in battle. It excites a Christian's spirits and makes him vigorous and lively in duty. What is done with cheerfulness is done with delight; and the soul flies most swiftly to heaven upon the wings of delight.

(6) If you would be violent for heaven, take heed of a *supine, lazy temper*. A slothful Christian is like a fearful soldier, that hath a good mind to the plunder, but is loath to storm the castle; so he would fain have heaven, but is loath to take it by storm. *Enerves animos odisse virtus solet.*[1] Sloth is the soul's sleep. Many instead of working out of salvation, sleep away salvation. Such as will not labour must be put at last to beg; they must beg as Dives, for one drop of water (Luke 16:24). An idle man, saith Solomon, 'puts his hand in his bosom' (Prov. 19:24). He should have his hand to the plough, and he puts it in his bosom. God never made heaven a hive for drones. Sloth is a disease apt to grow upon men; shake it off. A ship that is a slug, is a prey to the pirate. A sluggish soul is a prey to Satan. When the crocodile sleeps with his mouth open, the Indian rat gets into his belly, and eats his entrails. While men are asleep in sloth, the devil enters and devours them.

(7) Take heed of *consulting with flesh and blood*. As good consult with the devil as the flesh. The flesh is a bosom traitor. An enemy within the walls is worst. The flesh cries out, 'There is a lion in the way.' The flesh will bid thee spare thyself, as Peter did Christ: 'Oh be not so violent for heaven, spare thyself.' The flesh saith as Judas, 'What needs all this

[1] [Virtue has a habit of hating weak souls.]

OR, THE CHRISTIAN SOLDIER

waste?' So, what needs all this praying and wrestling? Why dost thou waste thy strength? What needs all this waste? The flesh cries out for ease. It is loath to put its neck under Christ's yoke. The flesh is for pleasure. It had rather be gaming than running the heavenly race. There is a description of fleshly pleasures in Amos 6:4-6: 'That lie upon beds of ivory, and stretch themselves upon their couches, that chant to the sound of the viol; that drink wine in bowls, and anoint themselves with the chief ointments.' These are the delights of the flesh. Such a one was he, spoken of in Beard's theatre, that did strive to please all his five senses at once. He did bespeak a room richly hung with fair pictures; he had the most delicious music; he had all the choice aromatics and perfumes; he had all the candies and curious preserves of the confectioner; he was lodged in the bed with a beautiful courtesan: thus did he indulge the flesh, and swore that he would spend all his estate to live one week like a god, though he were sure to be damned in hell the next day. Oh take heed of holding intelligence with the flesh! The flesh is a bad counsellor. St Paul would 'not confer with flesh and blood' (Gal. 1:16). The flesh is a sworn enemy to this holy violence: 'If ye live after the flesh ye shall die' (Rom. 8:13). You have taken an oath in baptism to renounce the flesh.

(8) Take heed of *listening to the voice of such carnal friends as would call you off from this blessed violence*. Fire when in snow will soon lose its heat, and by degrees go out. Among bad company you will soon lose your heat for religion. The company of the wicked will sooner cool you, than your company will heat them. Vinegar will sooner sour the wine, than the wine will sweeten the vinegar. How often do carnal friends the same to our souls as infected persons

do to our bodies, convey the plague. The wicked are still dissuading us from this violence; they will say, it is preciseness and singularity. As Christ's friends laid hold on him when he was going to preach: 'They went out to lay hold on him; for they said, He is beside himself' (Mark 3:21). Such as are unacquainted with the spirituality and sweetness of religion, judge all zeal frenzy; and therefore will lay hold upon us to hinder us in this sacred violence. When we are earnest suitors to piety, our carnal friends will raise some ill report of it, and so endeavour to break the match. Galeacius, marquis of Vico, being resolved for heaven, what a block in his way did he find his carnal relations, and what ado had he to break through that impediment![1] Take heed of a snare in your bosom. This is one of the devil's great subtleties, to hinder us from religion by our nearest relations, and so to shoot us with our own rib. He tempted Adam by his wife (Gen. 3:6). Who would have suspected the devil there? He handed over a temptation to Job by his wife: 'Dost thou still retain thine integrity?' (Job 2:9). What, notwithstanding all these disasters that have befallen thee, dost thou still pray and serve God? Throw off his livery, curse God and die. Thus would the devil have cooled Job's violence for heaven; but the shield of his faith quenched this fiery dart. Spira's friends stood in his way to heaven, for advising with them about Luther's doctrine; they persuaded

---

[1] Galeacius, or Galeazzo Caracciolo (1517–1586] was an Italian nobleman. A convert to the Reformed faith, he left Italy and settled in Geneva. An account of his life was written in Italian by Niccolo Balbani (Galeazzo's godson) which enjoyed widespread success, being translated into Latin by Theodore Beza, and later into English (1608), French, and Spanish.]

him to recant, and so openly abjuring his former faith, he felt a hell in his conscience. Take heed of such tempters; resolve to hold on your violence for heaven, though your carnal friends dissuade you. It is better to go to heaven with their hatred, than to hell with their love. It was a saying of St Jerome: If my parents should persuade me to deny Christ; if my mother should show me her breasts that gave me suck; if my wife should go to charm me with her embraces, I would forsake all and fly to Christ. If our dearest friends alive would lie in our way to heaven, we must either leap over them, or tread upon them.

(9) Take heed of *setting up your stay in the lowest pitch of grace*. He that hath the least grace may have motion but not violence. It is a pitiful thing to be contented with just so much grace as will keep life and soul together. A sick man may have life, but is not lively. Grace may live in the heart, but is sickly, and doth not flourish into lively acts. Weak grace will not withstand strong temptations, or carry through great sufferings: it will hardly follow Christ upon the water. Little grace will not do God much service. A tree that hath but little sap will not have much fruit. It may be said of some Christians, though they are not stillborn, yet they are starvelings in grace. They are like a ship that comes with much ado to the haven. Oh labour to grow to further degrees of sanctity! The more grace, the more strength; and the more strength, the more violence.

(10) If you would be violent for heaven, *take heed of this opinion that it is not so hard to get the kingdom; less violence will serve turn*. He that thinks he need not run a race so fast, will be apt to slack his pace. This hath undone many. Who will take pains for heaven that thinks it may be

had at a cheaper rate? But if it be so easy, what needs Christ say, Strive, as in an agony? What needed Paul beat down his body? Why doth the text speak of taking the kingdom by force? Is not conversion called a 'new birth' (John 3:7), a 'creation' (Psa. 51:10), and is that easy? Oh take heed of fancying that work easy which is both above nature, and against it! It is as great a wonder for a soul to be saved, as to see a millstone to be lift up into the middle region.

2. *Use those means which will promote this holy violence.*

(1) Keep up *daily prayer*. Prayer is the bellows that blows up the affections; and a Christian is most active when his affections are most violent. Prayer keeps the trade of religion a-going. Prayer is to the soul as the animal spirits are to the body; the animal spirits make the body more agile and lively, so doth prayer the soul. That the motion of a watch may be quicker, the spring must be wound up. Christian, wind up thy heart every day by prayer. Prayer fetcheth in strength from Christ; and when his strength comes in, it sets the soul a-working. Prayer leaves the heart in a good frame: as the morning sun leaves a warmth in the room all the day after. When Christians lay aside prayer, or leave off fervency in it, then by degrees they lose their holy violence.

(2) If you would be violent for heaven, *get under lively preaching*. The word is 'quick and powerful' (Heb. 4:12). It puts life into a dead heart. It is both a sword to cut down sin, and a spur to quicken grace. The word is a fire to thaw a frozen heart: 'Is not my word fire?' (Jer. 23:29). As good almost be without preaching as be under such preaching as will not warm. It is a part of the word, not only to inform,

but to inflame. 'Thy word hath quickened me' (Psa. 119:50). It is the lively dispensation of the oracles of heaven that must animate us and make us lively in our operation.

(3) If you would be violent for heaven *get your hearts filled with love to religion*. This is like the rod of myrtle in the traveller's hand Pliny speaks of, which makes him fresh and lively in his travel, and keeps him from being weary. When a man hath warmed himself at the fire, now he is fittest for work.

(4) If you would be violent in working out salvation, *warm yourselves at this fire of love*. A man will be violent for nothing but what he loves. Why are men so eager in their pursuit after gold, but because they love it? Love causeth delight, and delight causeth violence. What made St Paul labour more than all the other apostles? 'The love of Christ constrained him' (2 Cor. 5:14). Love is like oil to the wheels. Get love to religion, and you will never be weary; you will count those the best hours which are spent with God. He that digs in a silver vein sweats, yet love to the silver makes his labour delightful.

(5) If you would be violent *be vigilant*. The prophet stood upon his watchtower (Hab. 2:1). Why are Christians so listless in their work, but because they are so careless in their watch? Did they but watch to see how their enemy watcheth, they would be violent to resist him. Did they but watch to see how their time runs, or rather flies, they would be violent to redeem it. Did they but watch to see how their hearts loiter in religion, they would spur on faster to heaven. The reason there is so little violence in religion is because there is so little vigilance. When Christians neglect their spiritual watch and grow secure, now their motion to

heaven is retarded, and Satan's motions to sin are renewed. Our sleeping time is Satan's tempting time.

(6) If you would be violent for the kingdom *bind your heart to God by sacred vows*. A servant will be more diligent after he is bound to his master. Vow to the Lord, that by his grace you will act more vigorously in the sphere of religion. 'Thy vows are upon me, O God' (Psa. 56:12). A vow binds the votary to duty. He looks upon himself now as under a special obligation and that quickens endeavour. No question but a Christian may make such a vow, because the round of it is morally good; he vows nothing but what he is bound to do, namely, to walk more closely with God. Only remember, that we vow not in our own strength but Christ's. We must confide in him as well for strength as righteousness: 'In the Lord I have righteousness and strength' (Isa. 45:24).

(7) If you would be violent for heaven *be sure you make going to heaven your business*. What a man looks on as an indifference, or thing by the bye, he will never be violent for; but that which he makes his business, he will be industrious about. A man looks upon his trade as the only thing to get a livelihood by, and he follows it close: so if we would but look upon religion as the main business wherein our salvation is concerned, we should be violent in it. 'But one thing is needful' (Luke 10:42). This is the one thing – to get Christ and heaven. This is the end we came into the world for. If we could thus look upon the things of eternity as our business, the one thing, how earnest should we be in the pursuit of them.

(8) If you would be violent *have heaven continually in your eye*. This made Christ violent to the death; he had an

eye to the joy set before him (Heb. 12:2). Set the crown ever before you, and that will provoke endeavour.

Immensum gloria calcar habet.[1]

The mariner hath his hand to the stern and his eye to the star. While we are working, let us have an eye to that place where Christ is, the bright Morning Star. How willingly doth a man wade through a deep water that sees the dry land before him, and is sure to be crowned as soon as he comes ashore? Every time you cast your eyes up to heaven, think, Above that starry heaven is the empyrean heaven I am striving for. Thus did Moses: the eye of his faith quickened the feet of his obedience, 'He looked to the recompense of reward' (Heb. 11:26). When Christians lose their prospect of heaven, then they begin to slacken their pace in the way thither.

(9) If you would be violent for the kingdom *keep company with such as are violent*. When we want fire, we use to go to our neighbour's hearth and fetch fire. Often be among the godly, and so you shall fetch some heat and quickening from them. 'I am a companion of all them that fear thee' (Psa. 119:63). Good company quickens. The holy discourse and example of one saint doth whet and sharpen another. The saints never go so fast to heaven as when they go in company. One Christian helps forward another. In other races that are run, many times one hinders another; but in this race to heaven, one Christian helps forward another. 'Edify one another, even as also ye do' (1 Thess. 5:11). Oh let not this article of our creed be forgotten, 'The communion of saints'!

[1] [Glory is an immense stimulus.]

(10) If you would be violent, *never leave till you have the Spirit*. Desire of God to put forth the sweet violence of his Spirit. The spouse begged a gale of the Spirit: 'Awake, O north wind, blow, O south' (Song of Sol. 4:16). When God's Spirit blows upon us, now we go full sail to heaven. When the Spirit of the living creatures was in the wheels, then they moved (Ezek. 1:21). The wheels of our endeavour move apace when the Spirit of God is in these wheels. Seeing there are so many violent winds of temptation blowing us backward, we had need have the violent wind of God's Spirit blowing us forward to heaven. Let this suffice to have spoken of the means for this holy violence.

Concluding Applications

But may some say, *We have used this violence for heaven, what remains for us to do?* As the people said to Christ, 'What shall we do?' (Luke 3:10).

To aged Christians

You that have been violent for heaven (aged Christians), let me beseech you still to keep alive this holy violence. Not only keep up duty, but violence in duty. Remember, you have that corruption within you which is ready to abate this blessed violence. The brightest coal hath those ashes growing on it as is apt to choke the fire. You have those inbred corruptions, that like ashes, are ready to choke the fire of your zeal. How was Peter's grace cooled when he denied Christ! The church of Ephesus lost her keen edge of religion (Rev. 2:4). Take heed of declining in your affections. Be not like a body in an atrophy: be most violent at last. A stone, the nearer it is to the centre, the more violent it is in its motion. You have but a little time now to work for God, therefore work the harder. Be like the church of Thyatira: her 'last works were more than her first' (Rev. 2:19). Be as the sun that shines brightest before its setting, as the swan that sings sweetest before its death: 'Your salvation is nearer than when you believed' (Rom. 13:11). If your salvation be nearer, your violence should be greater. How should you quicken your pace, when you are within sight of the kingdom! He is a happy man of whom it may be said, spiritually, as of Moses literally before his death, 'His eyes waxed not dim, and his natural force was not abated' (Deut. 34:7). So a Christian's force and violence for heaven is not abated. He keeps the best wine of his life till last.

To violent Christians

Here is strong consolation to the violent Christian: thou art in the way to the kingdom. Though perhaps thou hast not a bunch of grapes in the way (I mean that joy which some meet with), yet it is happy that thou art in the way. Bless God that while some lie in the total neglect of duty, God hath given thee a heart to seek him: 'Let the hearts of them rejoice that seek the Lord' (Psa. 105:3). Nay, God hath not only given thee a heart to do duty, but to do duty mixed with love, which makes it savoury meat, and to do duty stamped with fervency, which makes it pass current with God. Oh bless God who hath raised thee off the bed of sloth, and stirred up the zeal of thy soul for heaven! He who hath made thee violent, will make thee victorious. Wait a while, and thou shalt be possessed of a kingdom. When Moses went up to receive God's commands, he stayed six days on the mount, and on the seventh day God called to him (Exod. 24:16). Though we wait long, and have not the thing waited for, yet let us continue doing our duty. Shortly, God will call us from heaven, 'Come up hither,' and we shall go from the mount of faith to the mount of vision, and behold those glorious things which eye hath not seen, nor can it enter into man's heart to conceive.

To fearful and weak Christians

But may a child of God say, 'I fear I am none of those violent ones that shall take heaven. I find such a deadness of heart in duty, that I question whether I shall ever arrive at the kingdom.'

This deadness of the heart may arise from natural causes. Weakness of body may occasion indisposition of mind. Thy prayer may be weak, because thy body is weak. A lute that is cracked cannot send forth as sweet a sound as if it were whole.

This indisposition of soul perhaps is only casual, and for a time; it may be in a deep fit of melancholy, or in desertion. When the sun is gone from our climate, the earth is as it were in desertion, and the trees are without blossom or fruit. But this is only for a time. Let but the sun return again in spring, and now the herbs flourish, and the trees put forth their fruit. So when God hides his face, there is a deadness upon a Christian's heart. He prays as if he prayed not. But let the Sun of Righteousness return, now he is divinely animated, and is as vigorous and lively in his operation as ever. He now recovers his first love.

Therefore, weak Christian, be not discouraged, so long as thou dost not allow thyself in thy distemper. A dead heart is thy burden. Look up to Christ thy high priest, who is merciful to bear with thy infirmities, and is mighty to help them.

PURITAN PAPERBACKS

1. *A Lifting Up for the Downcast* – William Bridge
2. *Heaven on Earth* – Thomas Brooks
3. *Sermons of the Great Ejection*
4. *The Mystery of Providence* – John Flavel
5. *A Sure Guide to Heaven* – Joseph Alleine
6. *Christian Freedom* – Samuel Bolton
7. *The Rare Jewel of Christian Contentment* – Jeremiah Burroughs
8. *The Sinfulness of Sin* – Ralph Venning
9. *Prayer* – John Bunyan
10. *Facing Grief* – John Flavel
11. *Precious Remedies Against Satan's Devices* – Thomas Brooks
12. *The Christian's Great Interest* – William Guthrie
13. *Letters of Samuel Rutherford* – Samuel Rutherford
14. *The Reformed Pastor* – Richard Baxter
15. *A Puritan Golden Treasury* – I. D. E. Thomas
16. *The Shorter Catechism Explained* – Thomas Vincent
17. *All Things for Good* – Thomas Watson
18. *The Doctrine of Repentance* – Thomas Watson
19. *Communion with God* – John Owen
20. *The Godly Man's Picture* – Thomas Watson
21. *Apostasy from the Gospel* – John Owen

PURITAN PAPERBACKS

22 *The Glory of Christ* – John Owen
23 *The Art of Prophesying* – William Perkins
24 *All Loves Excelling* – John Bunyan
25 *The Holy Spirit* – John Owen
26 *The Bruised Reed* – Richard Sibbes
27 *Learning in Christ's School* – Ralph Venning
28 *Glorious Freedom* – Richard Sibbes
29 *Justification Vindicated* – Robert Traill
30 *The Spirit and the Church* – John Owen
31 *The Lord's Supper* – Thomas Watson
32 *Come and Welcome to Jesus Christ* – John Bunyan
33 *Christian Love* – Hugh Binning
34 *The Mortification of Sin* – John Owen
35 *The Acceptable Sacrifice* – John Bunyan
36 *Dying Thoughts* – Richard Baxter
37 *The Jerusalem Sinner Saved* – John Bunyan
38 *The Secret Key to Heaven* – Thomas Brooks
39 *The Great Gain of Godliness* – Thomas Watson
40 *Temptation: Resisted and Repulsed* – John Owen
41 *Spiritual-Mindedness* – John Owen
42 *Indwelling Sin* – John Owen

PURITAN PAPERBACKS

43 *Smooth Stones Taken from Ancient Brooks* – C. H. Spurgeon
44 *The Love of Christ* – Richard Sibbes
45 *The Heart of Christ* – Thomas Goodwin
46 *Josiah's Reformation* – Richard Sibbes
47 *Christ Set Forth* – Thomas Goodwin
48 *A Heavenly Conference* – Richard Sibbes
49 *The Crook in the Lot* – Thomas Boston
50 *The Way to True Peace and Rest* – Robert Bruce
51 *All Things Made New* – John Flavel
52 *Flowers From a Puritan's Garden* – Spurgeon & Manton
53 *The Duties of Christian Fellowship* – John Owen
54 *The Fear of God* – John Bunyan
55 *Searching Our Hearts in Difficult Times* – John Owen
56 *Select Practical Writings* – Robert Traill
57 *The Incomparableness of God* – George Swinnock
58 *An Ark for All God's Noahs* – Thomas Brooks
59 *Preparations for Sufferings* – John Flavel
60 *The Glorious Feast of the Gospel* – Richard Sibbes
61 *Gospel Life* – John Owen
62 *Gospel Ministry* – John Owen
63 *Heaven Taken by Storm* – Thomas Watson

BANNER of TRUTH

THE Banner of Truth Trust originated in 1957 in London. The founders believed that much of the best literature of historic Christianity had been allowed to fall into oblivion and that, under God, its recovery could well lead not only to a strengthening of the church, but to true revival.

Inter-denominational in vision, this publishing work is now international, and our lists include a number of contemporary authors along with classics from the past. The translation of these books into many languages is encouraged.

A monthly magazine, *The Banner of Truth*, is also published. More information about this and all our publications can be found on our website or supplied by either of the offices below.

Head Office:
3 Murrayfield Road
Edinburgh
EH12 6EL
United Kingdom
Email: info@banneroftruth.co.uk

North America Office:
610 Alexander Spring Road
Carlisle, PA 17015
United States of America
Email: info@banneroftruth.org